STRANGE USA

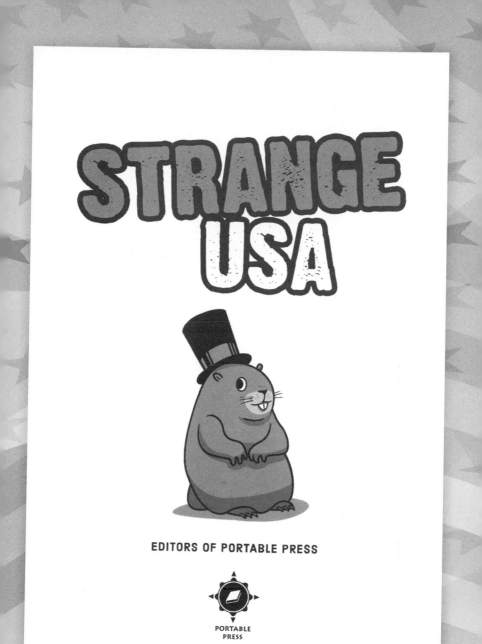

EDITORS OF PORTABLE PRESS

PORTABLE
PRESS

SAN DIEGO, CALIFORNIA

Portable Press
An imprint of Printers Row Publishing Group
9717 Pacific Heights Blvd, San Diego, CA 92121
www.portablepress.com • email: mail@portablepress.com

Printers Row Publishing Group is a division of Readerlink Distribution Services, LLC. Portable Press is a registered trademark of Readerlink Distribution Services, LLC.

Correspondence regarding the content of this book should be sent to Portable Press, Editorial Department, at the above address.

Publisher: Peter Norton • Associate Publisher: Ana Parker
Art Director: Charles McStravick
Senior Developmental Editor: April Graham
Production Team: Beno Chan, Julie Greene
Contributing Writer: Jay Newman
Cover Design and Illustration: Scrojo
Interior Illustrations: Scrojo

Library of Congress Control Number: 2022949394

ISBN: 978-1-6672-0053-8

Printed in India

27 26 25 24 23   1 2 3 4 5

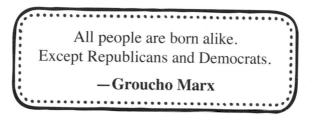

All people are born alike.
Except Republicans and Democrats.

—Groucho Marx

Introduction

God bless the strange USA! The editors of Portable Press sat down with Uncle Sam to collect the most interesting, odd, curious, and compelling facts about the people and places (and food) in this country we call home. The knowledge you'll gain here won't help you on a citizenship test, but you will find answers to the burning questions every patriotic American has surely asked— like who invented the corn dog, which Founding Father was the first to have indoor toilets, and just where Uncle Sam came from, anyway. Of course, not every story is about a famous figure or a well-known spot on the map. There are also plenty of tidbits about the odd, awesome, everyday folks who make up our fellow Americans.

From history to hauntings, from politics to pop culture, and from sea to shining sea, this isn't like any history book you encountered in school. After reading *Strange USA*, you'll have a new appreciation for America the beautiful—and bizarre!

STAR–SPANGLED GROANERS

Q. If April showers bring May flowers, what do May flowers bring?

A. Pilgrims.

Q. What was the American colonists' favorite drink?

A. Liber-tea.

Q. What did King George think of the American colonists?

A. He found them revolting.

Q. Where was the Declaration of Independence signed?

A. At the bottom.

STRANGE PLACES TO SPEND THE NIGHT

World Famous Clown Motel

LOCATION: A former mining town called Tonopah, in central Nevada

DETAILS: After Clarence David died, his children ended up with his collection of 150 clowns. They honored Clarence's memory by opening the Clown Motel in 1985. And clowns have been amassing there ever since. Today, there's a giant neon clown outside and thousands more clowns in the lobby's museum. Each room features "two to three custom clown art paintings."

For an extra $25, you can rent an EMF meter for ghost-hunting, because, of course, "America's Scariest Motel" is haunted. As they say on the website, "We'll do everything to make your stay comfortable, but what happens after dark is out of our hands . . ."

BE SURE TO . . . visit the Tonopah Cemetery, located right frickin' next to the Clown Motel. Most of the inhabitants of this Old West graveyard were killed in a mine fire in 1911. Nighty-night!

FIVE FREAKY FACTS ABOUT ...
PENNSYLVANIA

* The Philadelphia Phillies baseball team are the oldest continuous, one-name, one-city franchise in all of professional sports.

* Pennsylvania is the nation's second-largest producer of ice cream. (California is first.)

* It is illegal within the state to use dynamite to catch fish.

* The first public protest against slavery took place in 1688 in Germantown.

* Philadelphia was the first state to issue vanity license plates (in 1931).

Adventures of Florida Man

FIGHTING FIRE WITH FIRE

Two nights before the Fourth of July in 2021, residents in a Cape Coral, Florida, neighborhood were awakened by loud fireworks noises . . . kind of. It was one of their neighbors (unnamed in press reports) who was making the noises with his mouth: "BOOOOM!" "BISSHHHH!" "SPLLLLOODDE!" "FIRECRACKERRRRRR!" Police used security footage to track the Florida Man down and cite him for pretending to be a firework. He told the cops he was protesting against people who set off their fireworks early.

When Johnny Met Louisa

We often think of presidents and First Ladies as stodgy old men and women. But they too were young once—and the stories of how these power couples first got together show a human side to the presidency.

WHEN GEORGIE MET MARTHA

In 1758, Martha Dandridge Custis was 27, recently widowed, and a very wealthy woman. That year George Washington, also 27 and already a colonel in the Virginia militia—and not at all wealthy—met Martha via the Virginia high-society social scene and proceeded to court her. Courtship was quick, and they were married in January 1759, in what at the time was viewed as a marriage of convenience. They were, however, happily married for 41 years. (Note: the marriage took place at the plantation that Martha owned, in what was called the "White House.")

WHEN JOHNNY MET LOUISA

Louisa Catherine Johnson, who was born in London, met John Quincy Adams at her home in Nantes, France, in 1779. She was 4; he was 12. Adams was traveling with his father, John Adams, who was on a diplomatic mission in Europe. The two met again in 1795 in London, when John was a minister to the Netherlands. He courted Louisa, all the while telling her she'd have to improve herself if she was going to live up to his family's standards (his father was vice president at the time). She married him anyway, in 1797—and his family made it no secret that they disapproved of the "foreigner" in their family. Nevertheless, they were married until John Quincy Adams's death in 1848.

MICHIGAN ROCKS!

There's more to Michigan's musical heritage than Motown. Did you know these other rock 'n' rollers are also from Michigan?

ALICE COOPER

EMINEM

GRAND FUNK RAILROAD

IGGY POP & THE STOOGES

KID ROCK

MC5

TED NUGENT

MITCH RYDER & THE DETROIT WHEELS

BOB SEGER

THE WHITE STRIPES

POLITICIANS SPEAK

If I were two-faced,

would I be wearing

this one?

—ABRAHAM LINCOLN

STRANGE STATE SYMBOLS

Every US state has numerous official state symbols.
Here are a few fun ones.

ALASKA'S STATE FOSSIL: Woolly Mammoth

CALIFORNIA'S STATE FABRIC: Denim

HAWAII'S STATE TRADITIONAL MUSICAL INSTRUMENT: Pahu

IDAHO'S STATE HORSE: Appaloosa

IOWA'S STATE ROCK: Geode

NEVADA'S STATE ARTIFACT: Tule Duck Decoy

NEW MEXICO'S STATE COOKIE: Biscochito

NORTH CAROLINA'S STATE TOAST: "A toast"

OKLAHOMA'S STATE FLYING MAMMAL: Mexican Free-Tailed Bat

RHODE ISLAND'S STATE DRINK: Coffee Milk

SOUTH DAKOTA'S STATE BREAD: Fry Bread

TENNESSEE'S STATE WILD ANIMAL: Raccoon

UTAH'S STATE COOKING POT: Dutch Oven

RODEO LINGO

Rodeos are a staple event in the American West. But if you wanna be a rodeo cowboy, you'd better learn to talk like one.

ARM JERKER
A bull so strong it feels like it could yank the rider's arm out of its socket

BAD WRECK
(Is there ever a good wreck?) When a rider is bucked off hard and either horned or stomped on by the bull

BAREBACK BRONC
A horse without a saddle whose rider hangs onto a strap around the horse's ribcage

BARREL MAN
Also known as a "rodeo clown." The barrel man hides inside a barrel during the bull-riding event. If the rider is thrown, the barrel man springs into action to distract the bull from trampling the rider. The barrel protects the clown so he can protect the rider.

BULL ROPE
A flat braided rope that goes around the middle of a bull, which the rider hangs onto during the bull-riding event

CHAPS
The leather coverings that go over riding jeans.

COWBOY UP
Psyching yourself up, getting in the zone, or preparing mentally. Whatever your cliché, it's

getting ready to climb up and give it everything you've got.

CROW HOPPER
A bull that jumps stiff-legged, straight into the air instead of bucking

DOGIE
(As in, "Git along, little dogie.") An orphaned calf

FREE HAND
The one hand that must be free at all times during riding

FREIGHT TRAINED
If a bull sprints over a rider or barrel man and tramples him down, that person's been officially freight trained

GOOD BUCKER
A bronco or steer that gives a particularly feisty performance

HOOKER
A bull that throws the rider and attempts to hook him with his horns

HOULIHAN
A head-over-hooves somersault that a steer can make during the steer-wrestling event

SPINNER
A bull that spins in circles while trying to shake off his rider. It kind of looks like a puppy chasing his tail

SUCKS BACK
When referring to a bull, it's when he bucks in one direction and then quickly switches to another. When referring to a rodeo attendee, it means to quickly quaff a beer.

A Woman of Few Words

The Statue of Liberty stands as a symbol of hope, promising a better tomorrow to those who seek to make a new life in the United States. But the well-known verse that embodies that sentiment—"Give me your tired, your poor, / Your huddled masses yearning to breathe free"—wasn't added to the pedestal until 1903 . . . and then only after officials realized what an inspiration the statue had become to the waves of immigrants arriving at nearby Ellis Island.

The verse is part of "The New Colossus," a sonnet composed in 1883 by New York poet Emma Lazarus. She donated it to an auction at the New York Academy of Design to raise money for the statue's pedestal.

AMERICA'S STRANGEST RACES

Pig N' Ford

This race is held every August at the Tillamook County Fair on the Oregon Coast. When the starter gun fires, the racers run to a pig pen, grab a 20-pound pig, carry it to their stripped Ford Model T, hand crank the vehicle to start it, and then, cradling the pig in their lap, complete a lap around the track. Then they slide to a stop, shut off the engine, carry the pig back to the pen, get a new pig, run back to the Model T, hand crank it started, and do another lap. The first driver to complete three laps wins the race. This odd tradition began in 1925 after some farmers drove a pig to a farm and thought it would make for a fun race. Some of the original Model Ts still compete today.

HOT ENOUGH FOR YOU?

Death Valley is a place of extremes,
so here are five extreme facts about it.

☀ It got its name in 1849 from prospectors who
got lost taking a shortcut to the gold fields of
Northern California. After months wandering
thirsty and hungry in the desert, they finally
made it over the Panamint Range (near the
Mojave Desert) to safety. Amazingly, only one
person in their party had died. Still, on their
way out, one of them declared, "Good-bye,
Death Valley!" The name stuck.

☀ Average annual rainfall is 2.5 inches. In 1929
and 1953, no rain was recorded. Oddly, the
average evaporation rate is 150 inches. (No one
knows where all that moisture comes from.)

☀ It holds the record for North America's lowest
spot (282 feet below sea level) and hottest

place (record high of 134°F). (The record low was 15°F.)

☀ The most lucrative discovery made in Death Valley occurred in 1881, when businessman William T. Coleman discovered sodium borate, or borax, in the rocks near Furnace Creek. With many uses, including in detergents, fire retardants, and cosmetics, borax proved to be hugely profitable for Coleman, thanks to his Harmony Borax Works and the famous "twenty-mule teams" he used to haul it out of the desert between 1883 and 1889.

☀ The hot, dry climate is home to more than 1,000 plant species, more than 50 mammal species, nearly 350 kinds of birds, and fish, amphibians, and reptiles. Nearly all the mammals are nocturnal, to avoid the heat.

Super Ball Bowl

Super Balls aren't all bounce and no substance. In fact, the toy loaned its name—sort of—to a modern American sports institution. In the 1960s, when Lamar Hunt, founder of the American Football League (later part of the NFL), observed his kids playing with bouncy Super Balls, he thought up the name Super Bowl as a joke. (College football championships had been called "bowl games" since the 1920s.) When it came time for the first pro football championship in January 1967, no one had a better name for the game—so, for lack of a better option, the Super Bowl it was.

REGIONAL TREAT

ST. PAUL SANDWICH

FOUND IN: Chinese restaurants in St. Louis, Missouri

DESCRIPTION: It's a sandwich that consists of an egg foo yong patty on white bread with lettuce, tomato, bean sprouts, onions, dill pickle, and lots of mayonnaise. The origins of the sandwich—and its name—are unknown.

STRANGE TOWN NAMES

*Which US state is home to each
of these "Peculiar" towns? Answers on page 403.*

1. ___ ACCIDENT

2. ___ BAT CAVE

3. ___ BORING

4. ___ NORMAL

5. ___ PECULIAR

6. ___ RANDOM LAKE

7. ___ SANTA CLAUS

8. ___ DISH

9. ___ FUNK

10. ___ HURT

a. ILLINOIS

b. WISCONSIN

c. TEXAS

d. NORTH CAROLINA

e. NEBRASKA

f. INDIANA

g. MARYLAND

h. MISSOURI

i. VIRGINIA

j. OREGON

ROADSIDE MONSTERS

A T. REX IN OREGON

A 30-foot-tall T. rex looms over Highway 101 on the Oregon Coast. Even larger, peeking out from the trees, is a 46-foot-tall *Brachiosaurus*. Take a short walk through this old-growth rain forest and see 23 lifelike dinosaurs (or at least what the artists thought was lifelike when these were sculpted and painted in the 1950s).

PAUL BUNYAN AND BABE IN CALIFORNIA

Staring at drivers from the parking lot at Trees of Mystery, Paul Bunyan is 49 feet tall. His sidekick, Babe the Blue Ox, is 35 feet tall. Unlike most roadside monsters, Paul can talk (thanks to a speaker near his head and a cheeky staffer peering from a window above the gift shop). Paul likes to tell jokes and make fun of tourists taking selfies beneath Babe's big blue . . . er . . . male appendages. But the real stars are the Trees of Mystery, where you can stroll among some of the tallest, funkiest redwoods in the world.

A GIANT MIDDLE FINGER IN VERMONT

The giant middle finger (which lights up at night) cost Ted Pelkey $4,000 to erect. His motive? Revenge. After trying unsuccessfully for 12 years to obtain a commercial garage-building permit from the Westford Town Council—which ruled that an auto repair shop on his rural property would be an "eyesore"—Pelkey gave them a gesture they couldn't refuse: a 700-pound wooden hand (by local chain saw artist Charlie O'Brien) atop a 16-foot pole, with its middle finger pointing at the sky. It's art, so it's protected by the First Amendment, and the town council can't do a thing about it.

The finger has become a celebrity in its own right: it has a Facebook page, and it's featured in a short documentary called *A Very Large Gesture*, in which Pelkey admits, "Whether the finger's helped my case or hurt it, it's made me feel better."

WHY'D THEY CALL IT THAT?

Grand Canyon National Park, Arizona

The Grand Canyon's earliest American explorer, John Wesley Powell, was about to name a certain creek Silver Creek when he recalled a favorite hymn: "Shall we gather at the river, / where bright angel's feet have trod . . ." Since that day, thousands of feet have trod along the Bright Angel Trail.

Geologist and explorer Clarence Dutton took a more ecumenical view, and his names for monuments within the park were inspired by the religions and mythologies of the world: Vishnu Temple, Buddha Temple, Confucius Temple, Isis Temple, Wotan's Temple, Freya Castle, Hindu Amphitheater, Krishna Shrine, Apollo Temple, Zoroaster Temple, the Temple of Ra . . . the list goes on.

American Wit

When you're born,

you get a ticket to the freak show.

When you're born in America,

you get a front row seat.

—GEORGE CARLIN

Making Beautiful Music

In 1986, San Francisco artist Peter Richards and master stonemason and craftsman George Gonzales completed work on the Wave Organ, a sculpture that makes music when it's hit by ocean waves. It took six years for Richards and Gonzales to make first a prototype of the Wave Organ, then the organ itself.

The Wave Organ stands on a jetty at the eastern edge of San Francisco's Golden Gate National Recreation Area. The stone sculpture is made of carved marble and granite (many of the stones are headstones from an old cemetery that was demolished for new housing). There are also 25 pipes installed at various heights to catch the rising and falling tides. According to Richards, the best time to visit is at high tide, and be sure to listen carefully: the sounds the organ makes are subtle and quiet.

Meet Me at the Station

No one knows for sure how the Underground Railroad—the network of safe houses and covert routes used by runaway slaves seeking freedom in the North—got its name, but many historians accept this explanation: In 1831, slave Tice Davids made a run for freedom, slipping into the Ohio River on the Kentucky side and swimming for the safety of Ohio with his irate master following after him. The slave owner pulled his boat to shore only minutes behind Davids, yet Davids was nowhere to be found. Perhaps, thought the puzzled slave owner, Davids had escaped via "an underground road." The Ohio Historical Society, though, says it's more likely that an abolitionist—probably John Parker or John Rankin, both famous in Ohio for helping runaway slaves—met Davids and took him to a safe house.

AMERICA: HOME OF THE WORLD'S LARGEST . . .
ELEPHANT BUILDING

LOCATION: Margate, New Jersey

DETAILS: No, it's not the secret headquarters of the Republican Party. It's Lucy, the world's tallest elephant-shaped building. Located a couple of miles south of Atlantic City, the six-story-tall pachyderm was initially built in 1881 as a real estate office. In her lifetime, Lucy has also been a functional home and a neighborhood pub. Her ears are 17 feet long, her body is 38 feet long, and her head is 16 feet high. Made of sheet tin, the oceanfront elephant is now the only elephant registered as a National Historic Landmark, and today visitors can get a guided tour of its interior.

FARMER BILL DIES IN HOUSE

Check out these real US political headlines.

Rally Against Apathy Draws Small Crowd

Legislators Tax Brains to Cut Deficit

California Governor Makes Stand on Dirty Toilets

Reagan Wins on Budget, but Moore Lies Ahead

LEGALIZED OUTHOUSES AIRED BY LEGISLATURE

Massachusetts Woman Has Eye on Kerry's Seat

Elizabeth Dole Had No Choice but to Run as a Woman

Brawl Erupts at Peace Ceremony

Carter Plans Swell Deficit

Red Tape Holds Up New Bridge

WILLIAM KELLY WAS FED SECRETARY

Nation Split on Bush as Uniter or Divider

Hotel Cancels Jihad Conference, Citing Safety Reasons

HILLARY CLINTON ON WELFARE

Marijuana Issue Sent to Joint Committee

L.A. Voters Approve Urban Renewal by Landslide

Louisiana Governor Defends His Wife, Gift from Korean

Mayor Parris to Homeless: Go Home

Mayor Says DC Is Safe Except for Murders

Ten Commandments: Supreme Court Says Some OK, Some Not

Democrats Are Looking for a Weed Deal

Future Famous

Ellis Island, the immigration processing center located in New York Harbor, was the gateway to the United States for millions seeking a better life. The very first immigrant processed there—on New Year's Day, 1892—was 17-year-old Annie Moore, who'd left Ireland 12 days earlier with her two younger brothers to join their parents after four years of separation. During the next 62 years of operation, more than 12 million immigrants passed through the island, including these future famous Americans.

ISAAC ASIMOV (1923)	ELIA KAZAN (1913)
IRVING BERLIN (1893)	BELA LUGOSI (1921)
FRANK CAPRA (1903)	ARTHUR MURRAY (1897)
CLAUDETTE COLBERT (1906)	AYN RAND (1926)
MAX FACTOR (1906)	KNUTE ROCKNE (1893)
KAHLIL GIBRAN (1895)	YMA SUMAC (1946)
CARY GRANT (1920)	RUDOLPH VALENTINO (1913)
BOB HOPE (1908)	JOHNNY WEISSMULLER (1905)

American Bathing

AN EARLY AMERICAN "CLEAN"

In early America, a lot of people thought bathing was a health hazard. In 1837, Boston forbade bathing except on specific medical advice. In part, bathing was rare because preparing the bath was so difficult. Most people had to haul a tub into the kitchen, draw water from the well or spring, and heat it over a wood fire. The whole family might take turns using the same water until it became questionable whether the last to bathe was getting cleaner or dirtier.

WASHING IN WASHINGTON

During the presidency of John Quincy Adams, the presidential bathtub was the Potomac River. President Adams took his baths in the river just before sunrise. On one morning, someone absconded with the presidential clothes and Mr. Adams had to shout until he attracted the attention of a young boy who ran to the White House for more.

THE DUSTY TRAIL

Bathtubs were rare in the Wild West. In 1871, Tucson, Arizona, boasted 3,000 people, a newspaper, a brewery, two doctors, several saloons—but just one bathtub. Pee-ew!

Jefferson's "Air Closets"

Benjamin Franklin may be considered the nation's foremost inventor, but Thomas Jefferson, another prolific innovator, was responsible for one of America's earliest toilets. Jefferson enjoyed the luxury of flushing toilets—unheard of in the colonies—while staying in Paris in the late 18th century. Years later, he constructed three "air closets" at his home, Monticello: each was a small shaft, about as wide as was necessary for a seat, with a skylight above, and extending beneath the home's cellar into a "sink" lined with stonework.

It's not clear how waste was removed from these air closets, and there's no evidence of a flushing mechanism. One theory is that it was collected in a pot placed beneath each seat and then lowered into the cellar, where it was accessed and disposed of through a door in the passage wall. Another theory is that Jefferson simply had servants enter each room and remove the pots. One thing's for certain: the air closet was a much pleasanter alternative to the outhouse, which was the American standard at the time.

(The first American to have a flush toilet may have been the poet Henry Wadsworth Longfellow. He had it installed in 1840, and proudly showed it off to his guests.)

The Baking Icon Who Never Was

In the early 20th century, the Washburn-Crosby Company (later General Mills) saw their Gold Medal flour soar in popularity. After a successful ad campaign in the *Saturday Evening Post* resulted in a barrage of letters from women asking for baking advice, the company decided that each letter should be answered and signed with a common signature to make the interaction between company and customer more personal. So Washburn-Crosby created the perfect cooking authority. "Betty" was a popular first name at the time; "Crocker" came from a recently retired company executive (William G. Crocker). And so, in 1921, Betty Crocker was born.

Secretary Florence Lindeberg won a company-wide contest for Betty's signature, which has appeared on all Betty Crocker products since. In 1924, General Mills put Betty on the radio, giving a voice to the name. Her first print portrait appeared in 1936, when prominent New York artist Neysa McMein created a composite painting combining the images of numerous female employees of the company's home service department into a single motherly image. Betty's portrait has seen several revisions over the years—with hairdos and clothes that keep up with the times—but she remains an American icon.

Caesar the No Drama Llama

The summer of 2020 was a rough one for Portland, Oregon, with protesters filling downtown streets every night well into August. Then things started to calm down. Some of that calming can be credited to a llama named Caesar, who became

a welcome presence at protests because of his uncanny ability to put people at ease. The six-year-old, 350-pound, former "Argentine grand champion show llama" works with his 66-year-old caretaker—the appropriately named Larry McCool—who runs the Mystic Llama Farm in Jefferson. McCool told the *Washington Post* that Caesar is a "magical creature" and different

from other llamas (which are prone to being grumpy and spitting). "I don't care how big . . . [or] how intense that somebody is," says McCool, "it could be a big marcher in total riot gear, and he will come up and give Caesar a big hug."

When Caesar isn't de-escalating tensions, he's visiting special-needs kids and the elderly. But it was those ten Black Lives Matter protests in summer 2020 that made Caesar a celebrity—he now has nearly 15,000 Instagram followers. The question McCool gets asked the most is how he keeps the llama out of danger. "We've . . . heard the flash bombs going off, we've smelled the tear gas, but we make sure that we get out safely."

A CITY OF SUPERLATIVES

The Big Apple isn't the only big-city nickname.
For instance, there's . . .

CHARLOTTE, THE QUEEN CITY: Settlers named the
North Carolina city after the wife of King George
III of England, Queen Charlotte.

PHILADELPHIA, THE CITY OF BROTHERLY LOVE: A
reflection of the state of Pennsylvania's founding
by the peaceful religious sect known as the
Quakers, *Philadelphia* in Greek translates literally to
"city of brotherly love."

POLITICIANS SPEAK

The energy of the stars becomes us. We become the energy of the stars. Stardust and spirit unite and we begin: one with the universe, whole and holy. From one source, endless creative energy, bursting forth, kinetic, elemental; we, the earth, air, water and fire-source of nearly fifteen billion years of cosmic spiraling.

—Rep. Dennis Kucinich (D-OH)

STRANGE UNIVERSITY

Weird (but real) courses that have been offered at California colleges.

ARGUING WITH JUDGE JUDY: POPULAR "LOGIC" ON TV SHOWS
(UC Berkeley)

UNDERWATER BASKET WEAVING
(UC San Diego)

LEARNING FROM YOUTUBE
(Pitzer College)

THE UNBEARABLE WHITENESS OF BARBIE
(Occidental College)

THE JOY OF GARBAGE
(Santa Clara University)

THE SCIENCE OF SUPERHEROES
(UC Irvine)

THE SIMPSONS AND PHILOSOPHY
(UC Berkeley)

STUPIDITY
(Occidental College)

HANG 'EM HIGH!

Lynching didn't start in the Wild West, but had its origins during the American Revolution. A justice of the peace and a farmer in prewar days, Colonel Charles Lynch led a bunch of vigilantes to dispense their own brand of justice on British supporters and outlaws. Because of their efforts, hanging someone without a trial became known as "lynching," and bands of vigilantes bent on hanging their quarry were called "lynch mobs."

De-Merit Badges

*Move over, camping. Check out these strange
Boy Scout badges, past and present,
and the requirements for earning them.*

DENTISTRY. "Make a model tooth out of soap, clay, wax, or papier-mâché. Using a string and a large hand brush, show your troop or a school class proper tooth-brushing and flossing procedures."

AMERICAN LABOR. "Attend a meeting of a local union, a central labor council, or an employee organization."

WELDING. "Show that you know first aid for injuries or illnesses that could occur while welding, including electrical shock, eye injuries, burns, fume inhalation, dizziness, skin irritation, and exposure to hazardous chemicals."

NUCLEAR SCIENCE. "Obtain a sample of irradiated and non-irradiated foods. Prepare the two foods and compare their taste and texture."

RAILROADING. "Using models or pictures, identify 10 types of railroad freight or passenger cars. Explain the purpose of each type of car."

CONSUMER BUYING. "Check into how to buy a used car."

TAXIDERMY. "Prepare and present at least five skulls of birds or animals, each of a different species."

CEMENT WORK. "Design and mold in a form, a concrete window-box, garden jar, garden seat, sundial, or hitching post."

PULP AND PAPER. "Make a list of 15 pulp or paper products found in your home. Share examples of 10 such products with your counselor."

INVENTION. "Invent and patent some useful article."

TRUCK TRANSPORTATION. "Assume that you are going to ship 500 pounds of goods from your town to another town 500 miles away. Your shipment must arrive within three days. Explain in writing."

MINING. "Discuss with your counselor two methods used to reduce rock in size, one of which uses a chemical process to extract a mineral."

ROBOTICS. "Explain to your counselor the most likely hazards you may encounter while working with robots."

FIVE FREAKY FACTS ABOUT ...
TEXAS

* Looking for Spring Creek? There are 33 streams or creeks in the state with that name.

* The Dallas–Fort Worth Airport is larger than the island of Manhattan.

* Juneteenth—the celebration of the emancipation of slaves—originated in Galveston in 1865.

* State law forbids you from selling your eye.

* El Paso is closer to California (516 miles) than it is to Dallas (571 miles).

FOUNDING FLAVORS

While living in New York City in 1790, George Washington ran up a $200 tab at a Manhattan ice cream shop. (That's more than $6,250 in today's money.)

I Ain't Giving Back That Medal!

Mary Edwards Walker was an 1855 graduate of Syracuse Medical College and an early supporter of women's rights, particularly the issue of dress reform. Walker enlisted in the Union Army in 1861, but was refused a commission as a surgeon. So she first served as a nurse, then was promoted to field surgeon, and, finally, assistant surgeon of the 52nd Ohio Infantry.

Walker frequently crossed Confederate lines to treat civilians (or, according to the rumors, to spy on the enemy)—until 1864, when she was caught and sent to jail in Richmond, Virginia. After four months she was released during a prisoner exchange—and was very pleased to be traded "man for man" for a Confederate officer. She spent the rest of the war practicing medicine at a Kentucky women's prison and a Tennessee orphanage.

For her service, President Andrew Johnson awarded Mary Walker the Congressional Medal of Honor. But during what's known as the "Purge of 1917," the federal government acted on a congressional law revising the Medal of Honor standards to include only "actual combat with an enemy." Result: Mary Walker's medal

was revoked. The 85-year-old Mary refused to return the medal to the army and, according to her friends, wore it proudly every day until her death two years later. In 1977, President Jimmy Carter reinstated the award, and Mary Edwards Walker remains the only woman to be so honored.

A Giant Hoax

In 1869, at an upstate New York farm just outside the town of Cardiff, well diggers found what seemed to be the petrified body of a man—a man who was a 10-foot-tall giant. The diggers had been hired by New York cigar maker George Hull, a relative of the farm's owner. News of the amazing discovery spread quickly. Hull charged people 50 cents to take a peek at the giant. Experts cried fraud, but the public ate it up, and the body went on tour. The sign that accompanied the giant claimed that P. T. Barnum had offered $50,000 to buy it. (The figure may have been lower, but an offer *had* been made.) Hull refused to sell, so Barnum made his own replica of the giant and sued Hull, declaring the original to be a fake.

During the ensuing trial, Hull admitted that the giant was nothing more than an elaborate hoax, carved from gypsum and washed with sulfuric acid to make it look old. He had thought up the idea after an argument with a fundamentalist preacher. He wondered if he could convince the preacher that the "giants in the earth" mentioned in the Bible were real. Of course, there was the money-making angle, too. Hull came out of the deal some $30,000 ahead.

First in Flight?

In the 1880s, John Montgomery of San Diego, California, studied the physics of flight and the wings of birds so that he could build a successful glider. He learned that planes were more successful if their wings, like those of birds, were shaped like cones. In 1883, he tested a glider with wings that were curved toward the front like a gull's wings. He flew over a hill in Otay Mesa, just outside San Diego, and glided for about 600 feet. It was the Western Hemisphere's first heavier-than-air, manned, controlled flight . . . and it occurred 20 years before the Wright brothers' engine-driven flight in North Carolina. By 1905, Montgomery had built tandem gliders that were launched from hot-air balloons, flew at up to a 4,000-foot elevation, and could coast to a landing.

THREE SISTERS

Pittsburgh boasts the only trio of identical bridges in the United States. They're called the "Three Sisters" and span the city's Sixth, Seventh, and Ninth Streets. All three yellow suspension bridges were built between 1924 and 1928 by the American Bridge Company, which still has its headquarters outside Pittsburgh.

The bridges are better known by their commemorative names: the Sixth Street bridge honors baseball player Roberto Clemente, Seventh Street is named after artist Andy Warhol, and the Ninth Street bridge is named for conservationist Rachel Carson.

Spell Check

These are the six most commonly misspelled US cities.

1. **PITTSBURGH, PA**

2. **TUCSON, AZ**

3. **CINCINNATI, OH**

4. **ALBUQUERQUE, NM**

5. **CULPEPER, VA**

6. **ASHEVILLE, NC**

American Wit

Never ask a man if
he's from Texas.
If he is, he'll tell you.
If he isn't, no need
to embarrass him.

—Anonymous

STRANGE TRIP

THE NUN DOLL MUSEUM

LOCATION: Indian River, Michigan

DETAILS: In 1964, Susan Rogalski opened up her collection of 230 nun dolls to the public. Now containing over 525 dolls, making it the world's largest museum of its kind, the collection represents more than 217 religious orders in North and South America. In addition to dolls, there are dioramas of nuns at work and 21 life-sized dummies modeling Roman Catholic attire. In 1988, Pope John Paul II blessed Rogalski and her husband Wally "for helping to promote vocations to the priesthood and religious life through their doll collection." Located nearby is the Cross in the Woods Shrine, a National Catholic Shrine, where visitors have the opportunity to pray before the giant 28-foot-tall crucifix with its seven-ton bronze Jesus.

A LITERAL BUCKET HAT

National Park Service rangers are law enforcement officers who protect and preserve our nation's park sites. You might recognize them because of their badges, but you're more likely to spot them because of the iconic brown felt "Smokey Bear" hat that's part of their uniform. The hat not only protects rangers from rain, sun, and falling objects, but it's also designed to be used to carry water and fan campfires in a pinch.

THAT'S NO MOON

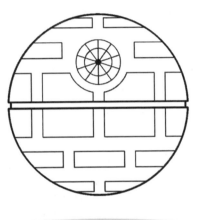

In 1988, college student Todd Franklin was at an antiques show in Lake of the Ozarks, Missouri, when he was drawn to a four-foot-tall gray ball that looked like the Death Star, the space station from the original *Star Wars* movie. Franklin called 20th Century Fox and was told the prop had been destroyed after filming. Not long after, the gray ball

was sold to nearby country music theater Star World, who displayed it in the lobby.

Several years later, while attending film school, Franklin talked to a *Star Wars* special effects artist, who said not all Death Star props had been destroyed. Franklin went back to Missouri, only to discover that Star World had closed and most possessions had been liquidated . . . but the ball was still there, being used as a trash can. A film historian who examined it verified that it was indeed the Death Star. After keeping it in his living room for a few years, Franklin sold it to a collector.

How did such an important piece of movie history end up in the Ozarks? It was stored in an Anaheim warehouse after filming. When the warehouse owners were moving to Missouri, they asked the studio to send someone to get their prop, but no one came. So they brought it with them, then sold it to the antiques store.

HOPE YOU MADE YOUR RETURNS

Here are six premier US department store chains that are now defunct.

1. **MAY**
2. **GIMBEL'S**
3. **WANAMAKER'S**
4. **THE BON MARCHÉ**
5. **MARSHALL FIELD'S**
6. **MONTGOMERY WARD**

Continuing Adventures of Florida Man

TONY TO THE RESCUE!

In July 2021, a lawn worker, whom police identified only as "Tony," was walking in his Palm Beach neighborhood. (However, Tony isn't the Florida Man in question.) Meanwhile, one of Tony's neighbors (also not the Florida Man) was driving by and started swerving. Tony saw the driver was convulsing, so he tried to stop the car, but it ran over his steel-toe boot before rolling to a stop in a nearby front yard. Tony frantically tried to reach the victim, but the door was locked, so he called 9-1-1, then ran and got the victim's wife. Rescuers reached the car in time to save the driver, and Tony was hailed a hero. So, where was the Florida Man? He was inside the house where the car had stopped, yelling repeatedly: "Get off our lawn! Get him out of here! Have him die somewhere else!"

America's Favorite "Pents"

Levi Strauss was an immigrant from Germany whose brothers owned a dry-goods store in New York. He carried their merchandise around in packs on his back, peddling it on the streets. In 1853, Strauss moved to California and set up his own dry-goods store in San Francisco. He built a local reputation for honesty, so when Nevada-based tailor Jacob Davis visited the city and wanted to start a business, he asked Strauss to be his partner. Davis had sewn heavy cotton work pants, or "waist overalls," that he made especially strong by hammering rivets in the pockets. In 1872, he pitched the product to Strauss: "The secret of them Pents, is the Rivits that I put in those Pockets . . . I cannot make them up fast enough." The pitch worked. Davis moved to San Francisco, and by 1873, the men were partners, manufacturing what came to be known as Levi's. Soon Californians were the ultimate trendsetters: they were wearing America's first jeans.

Batter Up...to the Bar

What was to become the New York Yankees began in 1903 when New York City bartenders Frank Farrell and William "Big Bill" Devery bought the struggling Baltimore Orioles for $18,000, transplanted them to New York, and renamed them the Highlanders. That gave the city two teams: the National League's Giants and the American League's Highlanders, who lost their first game, but made steady progress over the years. The team also started wearing pinstripes and took on the interlocking "NY" logo that was already being used as an honorary symbol for police officers killed in the line of duty. That logo has since become one of the most recognizable in sports . . . especially after 1913, when the Highlanders changed their name to the Yankees.

The Tan Suit Timeline

1950S: President Dwight D. Eisenhower wears a tan suit numerous times, but because pretty much everything is in black-and-white in the 1950s, no one notices.

JANUARY 3, 1959: Ike's vice president, Richard Nixon, wears a tan suit to the Alaska statehood ceremony. No one notices.

1978: President Jimmy Carter poses in the Oval Office for his official Presidential Portrait, wearing a tannish suit (in some photos it's more grayish). No one notices.

JULY 13, 1988: President Ronald Reagan and Vice President George H. W. Bush attend the signing of a proclamation. Both men are wearing tan suits. No one notices.

AUGUST 1, 1993: President Bill Clinton wears a tan suit to a service at United Foundry Methodist Church in Washington, DC. No one notices.

APRIL 3, 2004: Future President Donald Trump hosts *Saturday Night Live*. During a sketch called "Donald Trump's House of Wings," he wears a tan suit. No one notices.

AUGUST 28, 2014: President Barack Obama holds a press conference about the threat of ISIS. He's wearing a tan

suit. Lots of people notice. Rep. Steve King (R-NY) says the suit shows weakness: "There's no way . . . any of us can excuse what the president did yesterday." Obama critics come up with puns like "Yes We Tan" and "The Audacity of Taupe." Fashion magazines like *Esquire* call it a "monstrosity." "Khaki is sort of wishy-washy," writes the *New York Times*. The White House responds: "The president stands squarely behind the decision . . . to wear his summer suit . . . It's the Thursday before Labor Day. He feels pretty good about it."

2017–21: Donald Trump does not to wear a tan suit while in office. No one notices.

AUGUST 21, 2021: Two days after Obama's 60th birthday, his former VP, now President Joe Biden, wears a tan suit to a press conference. "Here in the East Room, I'm listening to the president," live-tweets BBC White House correspondent Tara McKelvey. "The subjects are serious— the economy, vaccinations, jobs—but it's hard to focus, since I was so distracted by his TAN SUIT."

POLITICIANS

SPEAK

I think this is the most extraordinary collection of talent, of human knowledge, that has ever been gathered together at the White House—with the possible exception of when Thomas Jefferson dined alone.

—JOHN F. KENNEDY,
at a White House dinner honoring
Nobel Prize winners

PARANORMAL PARKS, PART I

America's national parks are full of ghostly tales...

MELISSA: MAMMOTH CAVE NATIONAL PARK, KENTUCKY

According to legend, in 1858, a young woman named Melissa made a deathbed confession to having killed a man in the cave. It was an accident (of course!): Melissa had fallen in love with her tutor, but when he didn't return her feelings, she lured him into the labyrinth and then sneaked out when he wasn't looking. Melissa, a local, knew the cave well, but the tutor, from Boston, had no experience with the underground maze. Melissa waited for him to emerge frightened and contrite, but he never did. She claimed to have gone back after him, but no one ever saw the tutor again. After becoming sick with tuberculosis, Melissa fessed up to her crime and then died, still guilty over the tutor's disappearance.

Over the next 100 years, visitors to Mammoth Cave reported odd encounters they attribute to Melissa. One man spoke of hearing a woman calling out to someone in the deep recesses of the cave. And another visitor reported hearing what sounded like a woman's ghostly cough . . . Melissa had died of consumption, after all. Talk about a woman scorned!

Old Man of the Oats

German immigrant and Akron, Ohio, grocer Ferdinand Schumacher started selling oatmeal in his store in late 1854. Two years later, he bought an old wooden factory along the canal and started grinding oats. His company, called the German Mills American Oatmeal Company, could turn out 20 barrels of oats a day. Schumacher's company thrived over the next half century and earned him the nickname "the Oatmeal King"—business was especially good during the Civil War when the US government started buying Schumacher's oats to feed Union soldiers. In 1901, Schumacher's company merged with two other oat producers, Ravenna's Quaker Mill Company and a cereal mill in Iowa, to form the Quaker Oats Company . . . you know the one—it's got that white-haired man on its logo.

AMERICA:
HOME OF THE
WORLD'S LARGEST . . .
EGG

LOCATION: Winlock, Washington

DETAILS: A 12-foot-long, 1,200-pound fiberglass egg sits atop a steel pole right in the center of this small town just south of Seattle. In the early 20th century, Winlock was the second-largest egg producer in the United States, and the town built a giant egg to celebrate its claim to fame. The first egg was constructed from canvas in 1923. That egg was replaced with a plastic version in 1944, then with a fiberglass one in the 1960s. The local egg industry clucked its last cluck years ago, but the giant egg remains the centerpiece of Winlock's annual Egg Day celebration each June. Since 9/11, the egg has been painted like an American flag.

The First Woman to . . .

*These American women made history
with their achievements.*

FLY SOLO AROUND THE WORLD
Jerrie Mock: in 1964, she flew her Cessna, called *Spirit of Columbus*, from Ohio . . . to Ohio in 29 days, 11 hours, and 59 minutes.

SERVE ON THE SUPREME COURT
Sandra Day O'Connor: she was appointed a Supreme Court Justice by President Ronald Reagan in 1981.

BE ELECTED GOVERNOR OF A US STATE
Nellie Tayloe Ross: she became Wyoming's first (and, so far, only) female governor in 1925.

HOST A SYNDICATED DAYTIME TALK SHOW
Sally Jesse Raphael's long-running half-hour talk show debuted on a local St. Louis station in 1983. (Oprah was the first to go national in 1986.)

WIN A TONY AWARD FOR BEST MUSICAL SCORE
Although a few had won with a male collaborator, a woman didn't win it by herself until 2013 when 1980s pop icon Cyndi Lauper took home the award for her original score to the musical *Kinky Boots*.

WIN A NOBEL PRIZE

Jane Addams shared the 1931 Nobel Peace Prize with Nicholas Murray Butler. Addams founded the Women's International League for Peace and Freedom in 1919, and worked for international peace; at home in the US, she helped the poor, child laborers, and immigrants.

EARN A MEDICAL DEGREE IN THE US

Elizabeth Blackwell: when she applied to New York's Geneva Medical College (now called Hobart) in 1859, all 150 male students voted to accept her.

COMPETE IN A NASCAR EVENT

Sara Christian, at the first ever NASCAR Cup Series race (then called "Strictly Stock") in 1949. She competed against 32 other drivers and came in 14th.

VOTE IN A GENERAL ELECTION

Louisa Ann Swain. Wyoming (then a territory) granted some women the right to vote in 1869, and 70-year-old Swain was the first to cast a ballot in the 1870 election.

SERVE AS SPEAKER OF THE HOUSE OF REPRESENTATIVES

Nancy Pelosi. The California congresswoman served from 2007 to 2011, and again assumed the position in 2019.

FAST-FOOD FOUNDERS
In-N-Out Burger

NOW: There are more than 350 In-N-Out Burgers in California, Nevada, Utah, Arizona, Colorado, Oregon, and Texas. In 2021, the business made about $1.073 billion in revenue.

THEN: In 1948, the same year that McDonald's started using an assembly line to prepare its food, a different kind of revolution began in the Los Angeles County town of Baldwin Park. In-N-Out Burger founders Harry and Esther Snyder opened one of the first drive-through restaurants with no carhops, but with a two-way speaker box so people could order right from their cars. In-N-Out soon caused "burger jams," with cars forming a line out into the street.

Despite their success, the Snyders refused to expand rapidly or franchise. Instead, they insisted on overseeing the business to make sure that only fresh meat and produce went into their meals. When other restaurants began using frozen patties, Harry Snyder turned to a group of butchers who sold him high-quality meat. Instead of keeping prepared food warm, everything was made fresh, including the french fries. To maintain quality service, the Snyders trained employees well and paid high wages. Their emphasis on quality has turned In-N-Out into a beloved West Coast institution and made fans of famous chefs such as Gordon Ramsay and Julia Child.

Strange Places to Spend the Night

Dog Bark Park Inn

LOCATION: Cottonwood, a small town in western Idaho

DETAILS: "Look, kids, there's a giant beagle up the road!" If you hear this claim but there's no actual beagle, you may want to switch drivers. If there *is* a giant beagle, you're on US Route 95 in Cottonwood, where Dennis Sullivan and Frances Conklin's love of both dogs and chain saw art has grown to monstrous proportions. After making a pretty penny selling doggy sculptures on the QVC home shopping channel, the husband-and-wife team built a 12-foot-tall beagle on their property. But that wasn't big enough, so, right behind it, they built "Sweet Willy." At 30 feet tall, Willy is the world's tallest beagle. In 2003, it became the Dog Bark Park Inn. Visitors walk up a flight of steps to the living area in the dog's belly, then up some more stairs to a sitting room in Sweet Willy's head.

BE SURE TO . . . use the portable toilet out front. There's a regular bathroom located (fittingly) in the dog's rear end. But Dennis built a big fire hydrant around the portable toilet. It's very cute.

FAILED AMENDMENTS

Out of 11,000 proposed amendments to the US Constitution, only 27 have made it through the ratification process to become new supreme law of the land. Here are a few that failed.

NO TITLES OF NOBILITY (1810): "If any citizen of the United States shall accept, claim, receive or retain, any title of nobility or honor, or shall, without the consent of Congress, accept and retain any present, pension, office or emolument of any kind whatever, from any emperor, king, prince or foreign power, such person shall cease to be a citizen of the United States, and shall be incapable of holding any office of trust or profit under them, or either of them." This one was approved by Congress and is technically still active, but never ratified. (Meghan Markle, the Duchess of Sussex, might be grateful.)

THE U.S.E. (1893): Wisconsin representative Lucas Miller thought the United States would grow . . . and grow . . . and grow. He envisioned a republic that added state after state until "every Nation on Earth" had become part of the country. His proposed amendment: rename the nation "the United States of the Earth" in preparation for that future. Miller was not nominated for a second term.

NO MILLIONAIRES (1933): Washington state representative Wesley Lloyd wanted a constitutional amendment outlawing millionaires. He wanted income in excess of $1 million applied to the national debt. Congress did not agree.

NO BUDGET, NO PAY (2012): Most people understand that if they want to get paid, they have to do the work they've been hired to do. That's why Tennessee representative Jim Cooper introduced the "No Budget, No Pay" Act in 2012. Cooper's amendment prohibited paying any member of Congress (excluding the vice president) if both houses of Congress didn't pass the federal budget by October 1. Not only that, they couldn't receive retroactive pay for the period between October 1 and when they ultimately did pass the budget. It wasn't the first time Congress proposed punitive measures related to passing the budget. The 107th Congress (2001–2002) rejected an amendment that would have forced Congress members *and* the president to forfeit their salaries, on a per diem basis, for every day past the end of the fiscal year that a budget for that year remained unpassed. "Any other job in the world, you don't do your job, you don't get paid," Cooper said in 2012. "Congress shouldn't be any different."

Presidency? What Presidency?

From his early days as an assistant prosecutor in Ohio, William Howard Taft's dream was to serve as chief justice of the Supreme Court. But a career in politics got in the way. President William McKinley appointed Taft to the post of civilian governor-general of the Philippines in 1901, and President Theodore Roosevelt appointed him secretary of war in 1904. Taft was less than excited when Roosevelt tapped him to be the Republican presidential nominee in the 1908 election, but felt it was his duty. He won the election, but after serving an unremarkable four years, lost his reelection bid to Woodrow Wilson. Voted out of the job he never wanted, Taft dove right back into law. He later was appointed the president of Yale Law School, and then elected president of the American Bar Association. Finally, in 1921, Taft got his dream job when President Warren G. Harding nominated him to be chief justice of the Supreme Court. Taft served until just before his death in 1930, and wrote, "I don't remember that I ever was President."

Mega Monikers

Paul Bunyan may be the name of America's favorite fictional lumberjack. But get a load of these real lumberjack nicknames from the early 20th century.

ANGUS THE POPE

BATTLE AXE NELSON

BILL THE DANGLER

BUG HOUSE LYNCH

BLUEBERRY BOB

BUCKSKIN PANTS

CALICO BILL

CHARLEY THE LOGGER

CORDWOOD JOHNSON

CROSSHAUL PADDY

CRUEL FACE

DICK THE DANCER

DIRT DAN

DOUBLE BREASTED CORRIGAN

DROP CAKE MORLEY

FROG FACE

HAM BONE SMITH

HIGHPOCKETS

HUNGRY DAN SHEA

JACK THE HORSE

JIMMIE ON THE TRAIL

LARRY THE KICKER

LOUSY DAN

MOONLIGHT BOB

OLD RAMPIKE

ONE EYE

PANCAKE BILLIE

PANICKY PETE

PRUNE JUICE DOYLE

PUMP HANDLE

SILVER JACK

SQUARE HEAD

SQUEAKY GEORGE

SUB NELSON

STUTTERING ED

American
Wit

America's a family.

We all yell at each other,

and it all works out.

—Louis C. K.

REGIONAL TREAT

GARBAGE PLATE

FOUND IN: Rochester, New York

DESCRIPTION: Diner owner Nick Tahou (of Nick Tahou Hots) invented this dish in the late 1940s when some college students asked him for a plate with "all the garbage on it." The Plate starts with home fries and macaroni salad mixed together. It's then topped with two hamburger patties, onions, mustard, ketchup, and hot sauce. You can replace the hamburger patties with cheeseburgers, a steak, hot dogs, Italian sausages, sausage links, ham, or fried fish. The entrée is served at other Rochester restaurants, but since Tahou trademarked "Garbage Plate," it's usually listed on rival menus as the "Dumpster Plate."

This Old Shack

A bedroom or two, a bathroom or two, and a place to be a couch potato... that's all you really need, right? Not if you're a bazillionaire in California.

THE HEARST CASTLE

ADDRESS: 750 Hearst Castle Road, San Simeon

RICH RESIDENTS: William Randolph Hearst; his wife, Millicent; their five sons; and, occasionally, his mistress, Marion Davies

WHY IT'S FAMOUS: Possibly the most famous California mansion ever, the Hearst Castle took almost 30 years to build. Originally, newspaper magnate William Randolph Hearst intended to build a cabin on a stretch of land that his wealthy miner father left to him when he died, but ideas quickly spun out of control. In the end, the mansion grew to boast an airfield, a movie theater, a private zoo, 58 bedrooms, 60 bathrooms, and two swimming pools—one of which resembles a Roman bath and includes floor-to-ceiling mosaic tiles infused with gold.

CAN I VISIT? Yes. The castle is open for business and offers several types of tours.

FALCON LAIR

ADDRESS: 1436 Bella Drive, Beverly Hills

RICH RESIDENTS: Rudolph Valentino, Gloria Swanson, Doris Duke, and Joe Castro

WHY IT'S FAMOUS: Italian actor Rudolph Valentino rose to fame in the 1920s playing dashing leading men in movies such as *The Sheik* and *The Four Horsemen of the Apocalypse.* In 1925, he bought Falcon Lair, a mansion in Beverly Hills that he intended to share with his wife of two years, Natacha. But Natacha divorced him before the home was completed. Ultimately, Valentino used the home as a retreat and furnished it with fabulous antiques purchased during his travels overseas. When he died of a perforated gastric ulcer in 1926, Falcon Lair was sold to pay his debts.

In the 1950s, actress Gloria Swanson rented the place for a while, and then Doris Duke (heir to a tobacco and energy fortune) moved in with her boyfriend, jazz pianist Joe Castro. Duke was an antiques collector, and she bought all the pieces to Napoleon's original war room, shipped them to California, and set them up in the house just as the emperor had displayed them in the 1800s. Duke died in 1993 under mysterious circumstances, and the butler everyone suspected of killing her (by drugging her with morphine) was named a beneficiary in her will. He lived there until his death in 1996 . . . caring for the dogs Duke had left behind and to whom she had willed more than $100,000. After his death, the mansion was sold again . . . and again . . . but was never really renovated or kept up. Finally, it fell into such disrepair that the main buildings were demolished in 2006.

CAN I VISIT? No. The house is gone, but the property and the outer gates are still there.

Chocolaty Victory

The Hershey Chocolate Company helped Uncle Sam during World War II by supplying chocolate bars to the troops. More than 3 billion "Ration D" bars were manufactured and distributed to US soldiers between 1943 and 1945. By the end of the war, the Hershey factory was turning out the chocolate bars at the rate of 24 million per week.

COUNTER CULTURE

Diners evolved from early lunch wagons, which first began popping up in New England during the 1800s to offer low-cost meals to urban workers. Restaurant owners set up shop in mobile, retired trolley cars, street cars, or railroad cars and started serving food where workers congregated. At the turn of the century, there were so many lunch wagons roaming the streets that cities started requiring operating permits and restricted their hours of business. To bypass these rules, some owners started settling down in permanent locations where rent was cheap. Around 1923, people started calling these stationary lunch wagons "diners." By then, manufacturers had begun building them with restrooms and with more counter and table seating. In the 1930s, they got another makeover when longer, sleeker, stainless steel models came on the scene. After World War II, the diner business was booming thanks to postwar prosperity. Although the rise of fast food has affected the diner industry, these counter-serve restaurants are still a staple of American dining.

Birth of Uncle Sam

"Uncle Sam," the iconic personification of America, was modeled after Samuel Wilson, a meatpacker from the New York town of Troy. During the War of 1812, Wilson supplied beef to the US Army in crates stamped with the initials "U.S." to show they belonged to the government. When someone asked what the letters stood for, a worker at Wilson's plant jokingly responded, "Uncle Sam," a nickname for Wilson. As time went on, other products marked the same way were linked to Wilson, and "Uncle Sam" became a nickname for the United States as well.

Today, Americans recognize Uncle Sam by his top hat, coattails, and long white whiskers. But how did he come by this signature look? Uncle Sam's appearance stems from that of his two predecessors: Yankee Doodle, the moniker bestowed on colonials by the British during the Revolutionary War, and Brother Jonathan, a witty fictional personification of New England (who wore a tall hat and striped pants). By the end of the 19th century, British and American political cartoonists like Thomas Nast had helped define Uncle Sam's patriotic appearance and establish him as a symbol for the nation.

AMERICAN OUTBACK

Outback is an American restaurant chain. So why is it Australia-themed, displaying boomerangs and other "Down Under" memorabilia on the walls, and offering "Aussie-Tizers" on the menu? Because it was founded in 1988. That was right around the time when all things Australian became hot in the United States, thanks to media exposure, such as Paul Hogan's TV ads for Australian tourism ("I'll slip an extra shrimp on the barbie for you"), his 1986 blockbuster movie *Crocodile Dundee*, and Australian football player Jacko's popular battery commercials ("Energizer! Oi!"). Some Florida restaurateurs looking to open a steakhouse needed an angle . . . and they found one.

IT'S A CONSPIRACY!

Americans actually believed this?
Yep!

THEORY: George W. Bush was the inspiration for Curious George, and was willing to commit murder in order keep that a secret.

THE STORY: Little George Bush was a curious child who was constantly getting into trouble. Margret and H. A. Rey, friends of Bush's parents, wrote a series of books about a mischievous monkey whom they named Curious George after the mischievous boy. The books were immensely popular, but Bush didn't learn that he was the inspiration for the character (his father told him) until 2006, when he was already president of the United States. Facing low approval ratings and a public perception of being dim-witted, Bush was embarrassed and outraged. To prevent the information from leaking out, he ordered the Reys killed. When he found out they'd both been dead for years, Bush ordered the murder of Alan Shalleck, owner of the movie rights to Curious George and producer of the 2006 *Curious George* film.

THE TRUTH: It's impossible for Bush to have been the inspiration for Curious George. The Reys never met the Bush family, and they wrote their first book in 1939, seven years before Bush was born. Alan Shalleck was indeed a real person: He wrote several episodes of a *Curious George* TV series in the 1980s, but he wasn't a producer on the feature film. And he was in fact murdered, but not by Bush. Shalleck was found dead in his Florida home in February 2006, the victim of a botched robbery.

ATTENTION, LIBRARY SHOPPERS

During the Great Depression, the New York Public Library ran a store in its basement, offering groceries, food, tobacco, and clothing at reasonable prices. The two lion statues that flank the steps outside the library were named Patience and Fortitude by Mayor Fiorello La Guardia to remind New Yorkers that they could survive the Depression.

First American Thanksgiving

Massachusetts? Never heard of it. The first North American Thanksgiving celebration took place in Texas. In 1540, Francisco Vázquez de Coronado of Spain was appointed to explore the continent and seek out the "Quivira," a legendary city of gold. The expedition turned out to be a disaster—and a bad career move for everyone involved. The only gold Coronado found was in the West Texas sunset, and he lived the rest of his life as a desk jockey in Mexico City. (Yes, they had desks in the 16th century.)

But along the way, Coronado *did* find the first Thanksgiving celebration. On May 23, 1541, running low on both food and morale, Coronado and his men happened upon a band of Tejas Indians in Palo Duro Canyon (southeast of Amarillo), who gladly gave them both grub and a good time. A grateful Coronado declared it a day of giving thanks for this bounty in the new country. In 1959, the Texas Society Daughters of the American Colonists dedicated a plaque to the canyon, designating it as the place where the "first Thanksgiving feast" took place. And that makes it official.

Don't Trip on that Skirt!

George G. Anderson made the first successful recorded climb up Yosemite's Half Dome. He scaled the rock's 8,842 feet in 1875. Just days later, Sally Dutcher became the first woman to make the 17-mile round-trip climb—reportedly scaling the rock while wearing a long dress.

Today, thousands of people ascend Half Dome every year. Cables secured to the rock help modern climbers on the way up. Everyone from children to senior citizens has been known to make the climb. (But we doubt many of them are wearing skirts.)

POLITICIANS

SPEAK

It's clearly a budget.
It's got a lot of numbers
in it.

—GEORGE W. BUSH

Lady of the Lake

Many people from northwestern Pennsylvania swear they've seen a 30-foot-long sea serpent named Bessie living in Lake Erie. The legend began as early as 1817 but seems to have picked up steam since the 1960s. Fishermen often report hearing strange slapping noises on the lake, feeling something bumping against their boats, and even seeing a prehistoric-looking monster with scales. Most scientists insist that Bessie is nothing more than lore and claim that it's more likely the fishermen are seeing lake sturgeon, a type of fish that can grow to be four feet long and weigh 100 pounds. Sturgeon also have bony plates on their backs and barbels hanging from their lower jaws. Still, many people of the Lake Erie region remain convinced that Bessie is real—the Ohio city of Huron even offers a reward for her safe capture.

KODIAK ARREST

Humpy's Great Alaskan Alehouse in Anchorage offers this monstrous challenge: consume three pounds of Alaskan king crab, seven crab nuggets, 14 inches of reindeer sausage, side dishes, and a dessert of wild berry crisp and ice cream, all within one hour. It costs a whopping $250, but winners receive that money back, along with a spot in the Humpy's Hall of Fame and an "I got crabs at Humpy's" T-shirt.

Most people who finish do so just in the nick of time. Not Jefory C.—he crammed down the entire Kodiak Arrest (including the dessert) in only 12 minutes and 10 seconds.

WHY'D THEY CALL IT THAT?

Zion National Park, Utah

The views in Zion were heavenly to Methodist minister and explorer Frederick Fisher. He named a grand white sandstone monolith the Great White Throne because it resembled what he envisioned as the throne of God. He also named nearby Angel's Landing—a cliff so steep and treacherous that only an angel could land on it to bow at the feet of the deity sitting on the Great White Throne. The Three Patriarchs are three sandstone monoliths named for the three Biblical patriarchs, Abraham, Isaac, and Jacob. Fisher named a sheer white cliff with red stains running down its side the Altar of Sacrifice, an Old Testament reference. The Mormon pioneers got in on the name game, too: Kolob (as in Zion's Kolob Arch) is the star at the center of the universe—the star nearest the throne of God in Mormon doctrine.

Tax Dollars at Work

$ In October 2005, the US Department of
Homeland Security awarded a $36,300 grant
to the state of Kentucky. Purpose of the grant:
to prevent terrorists from using bingo halls to
raise money.

$ The Youth Outreach Unit of Blue Springs,
Missouri (population 48,000), received
$273,000 from the government to combat
teenage "goth culture."

$ In 1981, the US Army spent $6,000 in federal
funds in order to create a 17-page manual
for government agencies. The subject: how
to properly select and purchase a bottle of
Worcestershire sauce.

$ What did the US government spend $24.5
billion on in 2003? Nobody knows. According
to the General Accounting Office, that's
how much the federal government couldn't
account for that year.

Settling Nicodemus

In 1877, with Reconstruction in full swing in the American South, an African American pastor from Kentucky, W. H. Smigh, teamed up with a White land developer, W. R. Hill, to form the Nicodemus Town Company. Their goal: relocate African American Kentuckians to an all-Black town in Kansas. Of course, they first had to establish and build the town.

Kansas was a logical choice: it had been a free state and the home of abolitionist John Brown, and the US government was offering free land on the plains. By the summer of 1877, Smigh and Hill had persuaded 300 African Americans to move to 161 acres in northwestern Kansas. They named their new town Nicodemus.

By the mid-1880s, Nicodemus was a small but thriving town. Although there were many White-owned businesses in the town center, several others were owned and operated by Black residents. By the 1920s, more than 600 people lived in the town.

Today, Nicodemus is still populated predominantly by African Americans. It became a national historic site in 1996 and holds the distinction of being the only town west of the Mississippi River that was founded for and by former slaves.

The Magic's in the Mud

For decades, every new baseball used in the Major Leagues has had its sheen rubbed off with "magic mud" from New Jersey. In 1938, Philadelphia Athletics third base coach Lena Blackburne discovered the perfect muck for the task—sourced from an undisclosed mud hole along the Delaware River—and by the 1950s, the gunk was in use by every professional team in the United States. Before his death in 1968, Blackburne passed on the secret location to a friend, and Lena Blackburne Baseball Rubbing Mud is still produced to this day.

American Influence

★ In Spain, duct tape is called *cinta Americana* (American tape)

★ In France, brass knuckles are *le poing américain* (the American fist)

★ In Brazil, iceberg lettuce is *alface americana* (American lettuce)

★ In Slovenia, coleslaw is *ameriska solate* (American salad)

★ In Japan, a corn dog is *amerikandoggu* (self-explanatory)

★ In Italy, a placemat is *tovaglietta all-americana* (little American tablecloth)

★ The Dutch have a phrase that refers to the wage and advantages gap between rich and poor: *Amerikaanse toestanden* (American conditions)

As American as . . . Salad?

COBB SALAD. There are conflicting stories about who actually created this salad at Los Angeles's Brown Derby in the 1930s: the owner, Bob Cobb, or the restaurant's chef. Either way, the mixture of vegetables, diced chicken, eggs, bacon, cheese, and French dressing was named after Cobb and quickly became a staple all over the country.

CAESAR SALAD. The US gets only partial credit for this one. Caesar Cardini lived in San Diego, but in the 1920s, he built a restaurant just over the Mexican border in Tijuana to circumvent US Prohibition laws. The result was a steady stream of Southern California customers, and on July 4, 1924, Caesar's restaurant was so packed that he began running out of food. The solution? According to his daughter, he threw together a salad with what was in the kitchen: romaine lettuce, croutons, lemon juice, Worcestershire sauce, an egg, olive oil, and black pepper. He later opened a restaurant in Los Angeles and sold the salad there too.

RANCH DRESSING. Hidden Valley Ranch was a real place—a dude ranch outside Santa Barbara built by Gayle and Steve Henson in 1954. The Hensons created their own flavorful salad dressing so they could get their guests to eat inexpensive raw vegetables. The recipe

called for buttermilk, mayonnaise, herbs, and spices, and the Hensons got so many compliments that they started selling the herb-and-spice mixture in envelopes that guests could take home and mix with their own buttermilk and mayo. In 1972, the Hensons sold the recipe and the Hidden Valley Ranch name to Oakland's Clorox Co. for $8 million. First, Clorox added buttermilk flavoring to the mix so buyers could use plain milk, but in 1983, the company began selling the dressing in bottles. By 1992, ranch was America's most popular salad dressing.

GREEN GODDESS DRESSING. Credit for Green Goddess (mayonnaise, sour cream, lemon juice, pepper, anchovies, chives, chervil, and tarragon) goes to Philip Roemer, a former chef at the Palm Court Restaurant in San Francisco's Palace Hotel. In the mid-1920s, actor George Arliss stayed at the hotel and often ate at the Palm Court while he starred in a William Archer play nearby. Chef Roemer concocted the dressing as a tribute to Arliss . . . and he named it after the play—*The Green Goddess*.

Something for Everyone

The largest state-protected park in the contiguous United States, New York's Adirondack Park covers an astounding 9,375 square miles—an area roughly the size of Vermont. It houses the Adirondack Mountains, more than 3,000 lakes (including Lake Placid), more than 2,000 miles of hiking trails, thousands of miles of rivers and streams, and a huge variety of mammals, including black bears, moose, lynx, otters, beavers, and porcupines.

- Adirondack Park is larger than Yellowstone and Yosemite National Parks . . . combined.

- About 46 percent of the park—2.7 million acres—is a state-owned forest preserve, protected by the state constitution as "forever wild." The rest of the park is privately owned (mostly forest and sparsely developed farmland).

- There are 103 towns and villages within the park's boundaries, and about 137,000 people live there year-round.

- The Adirondack Mountains have 46 peaks more than 4,000 feet high, including Mt. Marcy, the state's highest, at 5,344 feet.

- There are no official entrances to Adirondack Park, and there is no entrance fee. Just drive, bike, walk—or canoe—right in.

American Wit

New York attracts the most talented

people in the world in the

arts and professions.

It also attracts them in other fields.

Even the bums are talented.

—EDMUND G. LOVE

STRANGE LAWS

* Using Silly String in Hollywood, California, could result in a $1,000 fine—but only on Halloween. Otherwise, have at it.

* There's a law in Deadwood, South Dakota, that prohibits the uses of psychic powers, including (but not limited to) "palmistry, necromancy, science cards, charms, potions, or magnetism."

* A Connecticut statute says you can't sell a pickle unless it bounces.

* Why *didn't* the chicken cross the road? Because it lives in Quitman, Georgia, where it's illegal for chickens to cross the road. (No word on *why*.)

* Attention, bingo players in North Carolina: bingo games cannot exceed five hours, so wrap it up.

AMERICA: HOME OF THE WORLD'S LARGEST ...

TIRE

LOCATION: Allen Park near Detroit Metro Airport, Michigan

DETAILS: A symbol of a once-booming local industry, this 86-foot-tall tire weighs 100 tons and was built to withstand hurricane-force winds. The tire was built as a Ferris wheel by the Uniroyal Tire Company for the 1964 World's Fair in New York. Two million people rode in its 24 gondolas, including Jacqueline Kennedy and the Shah of Iran. When the World's Fair ended, the Ferris wheel was dismantled and the tire was shipped off to Michigan, where it now sits, amusing tourists.

STRANGE TRIP

MÜTTER MUSEUM

LOCATION: Philadelphia, Pennsylvania

DETAILS: When it comes to weird museums, this one wins by . . . a bone. In 1858, local physician and professor Thomas Dent Mütter left $30,000 and a 1,700-piece collection of bones, plaster casts, and other medical-related items to the College of Physicians of Philadelphia to start a museum. The original museum opened in 1863 at the corner of Locust and 13th streets, but in 1908, when the displays outgrew their space, the college moved them to their current location on South 22nd Street. Today's exhibits showcase more than 20,000 objects, including a collection of brains, an Iron Lung, the "soap woman" (the body of a woman who died in the 19th century and was buried in soil containing chemicals that turned her remains into lye soap), and a plaster cast of history's most famous conjoined twins, Chang and Eng Bunker. But our vote for the strangest? It's a tie: a cancerous growth removed from President Grover Cleveland's upper jaw, and the thorax of assassin John Wilkes Booth.

The Curious Constitution of Stonewall Jackson

Thomas Jonathan Jackson was Robert E. Lee's most trusted lieutenant. He earned the nickname "Stonewall" during the first Battle of Bull Run, when his stoicism and confidence in the face of overwhelming odds caused his fellow general Bernard Bee to declare to his men, "Look! There stands Jackson like a stone wall." That rallied the troops and led to a rout of the Union forces.

But as brilliant as Stonewall was on the battlefield, he was also obsessed with his physical health. He was remembered by Ulysses S. Grant as a "fanatic" who "fancied that an evil spirit has taken possession of him." Colleagues at the Virginia Military Institute, where Jackson taught from 1851 to 1861, remembered him as a strange man constantly plagued by illnesses. By the time he entered the Civil War, his list of ailments—real or imagined—included rheumatism, chilblains, poor eyesight, cold feet, nervousness, neuralgia, bad hearing, tonsillitis, biliousness, and spinal distortion.

Jackson also had a few more nutty health superstitions:

★ Believing his left arm to be heavier than the right, Jackson would often—even in the heat of battle—raise

his left arm in the air to allow the blood to flow equally through his body and establish a state of equilibrium.

★ Terribly concerned about his self-diagnosed "dyspepsia," or indigestion, he maintained a diet consisting almost completely of fruits and vegetables. Whenever his troops overran Union camps, the general grabbed up as much fresh produce as he could.

★ He convinced himself that he would perform at his peak only when his bodily organs were stacked properly—in other words, in a bolt upright position. His study in Lexington, Virginia, had no chairs at all. When he did sit, he never allowed his body to rest against a chairback.

★ He suffered from poor eyesight for which he devised his own unique "treatment": dipping his head into a basin of cold water with his eyes wide open, staying there until his breath gave out.

Stonewall Jackson was only 39 when he died, and his death was fittingly odd: during the Battle of Chancellorsville on May 2, 1863, he was shot by his own troops in the left arm (perhaps he had it raised for equilibrium?). The arm was amputated and buried in a graveyard a mile from the hospital. When Jackson died eight days later, his body was sent home to Lexington for burial—but the arm stayed behind.

Spam-tastic

Hawaiians consume more Spam than residents of any other state: more than 7 million cans each year. Originally introduced to the state by GIs during World War II, it's become a staple of local cuisine. Hawaii's isolation means that canned, shelf-stable foods are an affordable alternative to fresh meats, and Spam's versatility makes it easy to incorporate into lots of dishes—like Spam fried rice and Spam loco moco (a breakfast dish with Spam, rice, egg, and gravy). The overwhelming local favorite: Spam musubi, a kind of Spam sushi. Here is how one aficionado describes the dish:

> Well, you take a slice of fried Spam, which has been marinated in a special sauce, place it on top of formed and sticky sushi rice and wrap a piece of seaweed, or nori, around it to hold it all together. It's like sushi. OK, it's pretty much like sushi. Except it's not fish. And the Spam is fried. So you can't call it raw. Which makes it not so much like sushi. But whatever . . .

That "Commonwealth" Thing

What do Kentucky, Massachusetts, Pennsylvania, and Virginia have in "common"? Each is a commonwealth, not a state. But what does that mean, exactly? Well . . . not much. A "commonwealth" is a political entity with a government that operates for the common weal (the common good), rather than to benefit the rulers (such as a king). This was a revolutionary idea in the 17th century, particularly for the British. The term was commonly used during the American Revolution because it signified that a state's residents saw themselves as having a government legitimized by the people, rather than by a monarchy. These four commonwealths are "commonwealths" instead of "states" simply because their constitutions call them that—at the time they were originally written, it was the preferred word. But in practical terms, they function like any other state in the union.

Youngest President?

There's some argument over who the youngest president has been: it all depends on which hairs you split. If you're interested in the youngest sitting president, then Teddy Roosevelt is your guy. He was just 42 years and 10 months old when he took office after President McKinley's death. But if you're talking the youngest *elected* president, then it's John F. Kennedy. When he took the oath of office in 1961, Jack was 43 years and 236 days old. (The oldest president? Joe Biden, who took office at 78 years and 61 days old.)

CALIFORNIA'S GOLD RUSH BY THE NUMBERS

1: Percent of the American population that migrated to California between 1848 and 1854. That's about 285,000 people, the largest free migration in US history. (The population of San Francisco alone soared from 459 in 1847 to 100,000 in 1849.)

3: Number of months it took prospectors to get their clean clothes back before Wah Lee opened San Francisco's first Chinese laundry in 1851. Prior to that, there were so few laundries that miners sent dirty clothes by ship to Hong Kong, where they were cleaned, pressed, and then shipped back.

7: Total Chinese population of California in 1848. The number rose to 11,794 by 1852 as immigrants flooded to the gold fields.

$16: Cost of a can of sardines in a typical California mining camp in 1849 ($585 today). In 1849, an ounce of gold also brought in about $16.

30: Percent of prospectors who died from disease, accidents, or violence between 1848 and 1852.

160: Weight, in pounds, of the largest gold "nugget" discovered during the California gold rush. The massive nugget was found in Calaveras County in 1854.

200: Number of deserted ships in San Francisco Bay on June 4, 1849. The crews had all abandoned them to seek their fortunes in the gold fields.

MAINE SLANG

Ever been "Down East" to Maine? The local accent and the local vernacular can make Maine-speak sound almost like a foreign language. In case you need it, here's our decoder guide.

AYUH Yes

BUGGIN' Lobster fishing

FINEST KIND The absolute best

CHOUT A contraction of "Watch out!"

THE COUNTRY The northernmost and most rural part of Maine—Aroostook County, where there's a large French-speaking population (it's close to Quebec)

CRITTAHS Animals

CUNNIN' Cute

DITE A small amount of something

DOORYARD The area in front of someone's house

DOWN CELLAH A basement

FROM AWAY If you're not from Maine, you're "from away"

GAWMY Awkward

I KNOW IT The equivalent of "You can say that again!"

ITALIANS Submarine sandwiches

KIFE To steal

NUMB Dumb

OUT IN THE WILLIE-WACKS To be out in the wilderness or the middle of nowhere

PRAYER HANDLES Your knees

PUCKAHBRUSH Vacant, undeveloped land covered in weeds

PUT ON A CORN SWEAT To try extremely hard

RIGHT OUT STRAIGHT To be very busy

RUGGED Stocky or thick of build (and meant as a compliment)

SAVAGE Anything that's fantastic or appreciated

SPLEENY Annoying and wimpy

STOVE-UP To wreck or destroy something

UGLY Angry

YOW'UN Kids or teenagers

MEET MR. ELASTIC

You know how the X-Men discover their mutant powers when they become teenagers? That sort of happened to Moses Lanham—though his particular "superpower" wouldn't thwart any supervillains. In 1975, the 14-year-old Michigander was climbing a rope in gym class when he fell nearly 20 feet. His classmates recoiled when they saw both of Lanham's feet pointing *behind* him. But that wasn't all the result of the fall. Lanham was born with extra leg cartilage and tissue. Result: his feet can turn 180 degrees. Does it hurt? "It's actually more comfortable," he said. Can he walk like that? Yes, and quickly. Lanham earned a spot in Guinness World Records for "Fastest time to walk 20 m with feet facing backwards: 19.59 seconds."

Lanham and his backward feet have appeared in movies and on TV (he was part of a freak

show in *The X-Files*). He was also featured on
Stan Lee's Superhumans and *America's Got Talent*.
Mr. Elastic retired from contortionism in 2018,
after a fall down a flight of steps while filming a
role in the horror movie *Candy Corn* resulted in
his no longer being able to turn his feet around.
But his son has inherited some of that extra
cartilage, although he can't walk as easily as his
dad. Maybe if he fell from a rope . . .

POLITICIANS SPEAK

I do think that Avatar told the truth, the whole truth, and nothing but the truth about some very serious socioeconomic realities in our world today. James Cameron was able to transmit such profound truths in cartoon form.

—Marianne Williamson,
2020 Democratic presidential nominee

AMERICA'S STRANGEST RACES

Train Racing

No actual trains are involved in this type of race, held in Denver. It's more like *The Human Centipede* . . . but with cars. Each "racer" consists of three cars chained together front to back. Only the first car has a motor—it steers and pulls the other two cars—but it has no brakes. The middle car is completely gutted; there's not even a driver. There is a driver in the third car, who assists with steering and does all the braking. That's an important job, as these car-i-pedes can reach speeds of 60 miles per hour as they whip their "tails" around the figure-eight track. Collisions are common, which is why this is often the final event at smash-up derbies.

Continuing Adventures of Florida Man

BAD BOY!

A Florida Man jumped in a parked car in a Port St. Lucie neighborhood and started doing doughnuts—backward—in a cul-de-sac. Wait, scratch that . . . it was actually a Florida *dog* (unnamed in press reports). Details are fuzzy as to whether the black Lab was already in the running car, or jumped in. Whichever it was, the owner had stepped away, and the dog kept driving in circles—taking out a mailbox and some garbage cans—long enough for police to arrive and put a stop to the mayhem. "When the cops got the door open [and] a black dog jumped out," said neighbor Anne Sabol, "I was like they should give that thing a license."

FIVE FREAKY FACTS ABOUT ...
NEW YORK

* Rochester was the birthplace of America's first gold tooth.

* According to a University of Massachusetts study, New York City bedbugs are 250 times more resistant to standard pesticides than Florida bedbugs.

* In Brooklyn, it is illegal for donkeys to sleep in bathtubs.

* New York City is technically an archipelago, not an island.

* Move over, Texas! Deep Hollow Ranch on Montauk, Long Island, is the oldest operating cattle ranch in the United States.

"The Hiking Sucks"

Proving you can't please everybody, here are some one-star Yelp reviews of some of America's most treasured national parks and monuments.

HAWAI'I VOLCANOES NATIONAL PARK: "Paid $20 to get in. Didn't even get to touch lava."

CRATER LAKE: "OK yes the water is very blue. And then also the water is quite blue, not to mention that the water is very blue. Other than that, mosquitoes ate the whole family alive, we left after one hour."

HALEAKALA: "Do yourself a favor and just google 'pretty sunrise' and save yourself the disappointment."

YELLOWSTONE: "If you've seen one geyser, you've seen them all."

BADLANDS: "I didn't see what the big deal was. We drove a million years to see some semi impressive rock formations? And there were RATTLESNAKES everywhere? Dumb. You lose cell service because you're in Nowhere USA. The only thing bad about these lands is entire experience. Waste of time. Thank god I was drunk in the backseat for the majority of the trip."

YOSEMITE: "How about you cut down the surrounding burned trees and make another parking lot or five."

ZION: "Picture a bunch of fraternity and sorority folks at Six Flags or Disney World and you will get an idea of what Zion is truly like in the summer."

BIG BEND: "I visited last year around Labor Day weekend. I thought there'd be lot of visitors and tourists but I was wrong. The park was empty. I found it lonely."

GRAND CANYON: "Every 500 feet a new vantage point of the same thing: a really big hole in the ground."

PETRIFIED FOREST: "Literally more petrified wood at the gift shop than in this entire 'forest.'"

SEQUOIA: "There are bugs and stuff, and they will bite you on your face."

DENALI: "DON'T TAKE THE BUS . . . drive the 19 miles in with your car. You'll see just as much and you don't have to listen to stupid tourists run their mouths all day."

DEATH VALLEY: "This is the ugliest place I've ever seen."

DEVIL'S TOWER: "Just a large elevated rock in the middle of nowhere."

CARLSBAD CAVERNS: "A walk along dimly lit paths with rocks and pits and pools illuminated BFD. If you have never been inside a cave or seen a picture of a cave this might interest you, otherwise don't waste your time, energy nor money."

JOSHUA TREE: "Ugly and the hiking sucks."

Makin' Bacon

It's no secret Americans love bacon—we eat more than 5.6 billion pounds each year. These are the top 10 US bacon markets.

1. **NEW YORK**
2. **LOS ANGELES**
3. **SAN ANTONIO**
4. **BALTIMORE/WASHINGTON, DC**
5. **CHICAGO**
6. **PHILADELPHIA**
7. **HOUSTON**
8. **CHARLESTON**
9. **FORT WORTH**
10. **ATLANTA**

Dead on the Fourth of July

The lives of the Founding Fathers were intertwined in many ways, none more so than those of John Adams and Thomas Jefferson. What had begun as a spirited friendship was almost destroyed by vicious political rivalries: after a bitter defeat in the 1800 presidential election, Adams skipped Jefferson's inauguration. The two didn't speak for another ten years, but in 1812, they decided to let bygones be bygones and struck up one of the most memorable correspondences in US history.

As their lives were intertwined, so were their deaths. Both the second and third presidents died on the same day: July 4, 1826, the 50th anniversary of the signing of the Declaration of Independence. Adams—92 at the time of his death—had vowed to live until the Jubilee of the nation's birth. His last words were "Thomas Jefferson survives." Little did he know, Jefferson himself had died earlier that day at Monticello.

Five years later, another president also died on the nation's birthday. The fifth president, James Monroe, died on July 4, 1831. On a happier note, one president was born on the Fourth of July: Calvin Coolidge, the 30th president, was born on July 4, 1872.

MISTER ROGERS' PITTSBURGH

Fred McFeely Rogers (better known as Mister Rogers) was born in Latrobe, Pennsylvania, in 1928. Forty years later, he was the host of one of the most popular children's programs in history: *Mister Rogers' Neighborhood*. The show began in 1968 in Pittsburgh and was first broadcast locally; in 1970, PBS picked it up for national distribution. Even as *Mister Rogers' Neighborhood* was beamed into homes all over the United States, it continued to be filmed at WQED studios in Pittsburgh and stayed there for its entire 33-year run.

One of the show's best-known segments is "The Land of Make Believe," which is populated with puppets and can be accessed only by a magical trolley. But Rogers didn't just imagine that trolley: it was based on one in Pittsburgh that he'd loved riding while he was growing up.

That Invention Didn't Suck!

James Spangler, a Canton, Ohio, department store janitor, invented the electric vacuum cleaner in 1907. He did so to make his own job easier. Originally, the dust bag was a pillowcase, and the rest of the machine was made of wood and tin. Because Spangler lacked resources to mass-produce his invention, he asked his childhood friend to help him out. That friend? William Hoover.

Honky-Tonk Heaven

It's no surprise that Texas lays claim to the world's largest honky-tonk. Billy Bob's Texas, in Fort Worth, covers a whopping 100,000 square feet. That's enough space for up to 6,000 country-music fans to congregate—and they can quench their thirst at one of the hall's more than 30 bars. While plenty of venues feature mechanical bull riding, patrons of Billy Bob's can watch professional and semi-pro rodeo athletes ride real bulls in an arena located within the club. Before it was a honky-tonk, the building was, at different times, a barn, an airplane factory, and a department store so large that stock boys did their job on roller skates.

THE "NEW" WEST

When did the Old West come to an official end? Some sources say as early as the 1890s, when the mass migration westward had slowed to a trickle, while others put it at 1912, when the additions of Arizona and New Mexico completed the contiguous United States as we know it today. But even as recently as a century ago, much of the western United States still had that wild, frontier feeling. The last stagecoach robbery occurred in Jarbidge, Nevada, in 1916, and the last train robbery occurred in Oregon in 1923. But it was in 1924, after several Apache were arrested for stealing some horses in Arizona, that the Indian Wars were declared over. With that, the West was finally won.

FIVE FREAKY FACTS ABOUT...
MT. RUSHMORE

* The four faces in Mt. Rushmore are scaled to men who would stand 465 feet tall.

* 450,000 tons of rock were cut away and still lie at the base of the mountain.

* Each head is 60 feet high, each nose 20 feet long, each mouth 18 feet wide, each eye 11 feet across.

* There are two-foot shafts cut in the center of each pupil in order to catch the light to make a glint.

* Some grumbled about the sculptor's choice to include Theodore Roosevelt, since Teddy and the artist were personal friends.

Shoot on a Shingle

American **GI**s had to do something to make
their chow palatable. Can you match the various food
and drink items (1–14) with the slang terms (a–n) that
World War II soldiers invented for them?
For answers, turn to page 403.

1. ____ BEANS

2. ____ BREAD

3. ____ CANNED MILK

4. ____ COFFEE

5. ____ CRACKERS

6. ____ GRAPE NUTS

7. ____ HASH

8. ____ KETCHUP

9. ____ MAPLE SYRUP

10. ____ MEAT LOAF

11. ____ PANCAKES

12. ____ POWDERED MILK

13. ____ SALT AND PEPPER

14. ____ SOUP

a. AMMUNITION

b. ARMORED COW

c. CHALK

d. DOG BISCUITS

e. GUN WADDING

f. HOT WATER

g. MACHINE OIL

h. MYSTERY PLATE

i. BATTERY ACID

j. PTOMAINE STEAK

k. RUBBER PATCHES

l. SAND AND DIRT

m. SHRAPNEL

n. TRANSFUSION

CEMETERY OF THE STARS

Visit your favorite celebrities at the Hollywood Forever Cemetery in Los Angeles.

FAMOUS "RESIDENTS": Movie lovers often visit the graves of Rudolph Valentino, Douglas Fairbanks, Jayne Mansfield, Faye Wray (without King Kong), and Marion Davies (mostly famous for being William Randolph Hearst's mistress). There's also a memorial to African American actress Hattie McDaniel, who won an Oscar for playing Mammy in *Gone With the Wind*. Unfortunately, McDaniel's tomb is empty; she wanted to be buried here, but she was excluded because of her race. Young hipsters pay their respects to punk rocker Johnny Ramone, whose grave includes a life-size statue of him wailing on the guitar. Another famous stop is the grave of Mel Blanc, the voice of Bugs Bunny—his headstone reads "That's All Folks."

CLAIM TO FAME: Established in 1899, the cemetery was *the* place to be buried from the 1920s through the late 1940s. These days, Hollywood Forever has more than just famous corpses. It boasts all kinds of activities: On summer evenings, thousands of visitors

come with blankets and picnic baskets to watch movies screened on the white mausoleum walls. There are concerts on weekends, and annual Day of the Dead celebrations feature sacred ceremonial tributes, musical entertainment, and lots of gourmet Mexican food. Hollywood Forever is also (we hope) the only cemetery in the country that's recommended by local magazines as a great place to bring a date.

Madison Square Garden Did It First

Here are some of the fantastic firsts that have happened at the "World's Most Famous Arena" since it opened in New York in 1974.

NORTH AMERICA'S FIRST ARTIFICIAL ICE RINK: On February 12, 1879, a 6,000-square-foot ice rink was installed to coincide with a gala ice carnival attracting thousands of revelers to the arena.

FIRST INDOOR FOOTBALL GAME: The inaugural game of the World Series of Pro Football saw Syracuse defeat New York on December 28, 1902.

FIRST TELEVISED BASKETBALL GAME: Only one camera was used to broadcast the Fordham University Rams defeat the University of Pittsburgh Panthers on February 28, 1940.

FIRST SPECIAL BENEFIT CONCERT: The Concert for Bangladesh, on August 1, 1971, featured acts such as Eric Clapton and Bob Dylan, and raised money for Bangladeshi refugees.

FIRST WRESTLEMANIA: On March 31, 1985, nine matches—including one featuring the much-hyped tag team of Hulk Hogan and Mr. T—took place during "the greatest wrestling event of all time."

FIRST HDTV SCOREBOARD: At the New York Rangers' home opener in October 2000, the Garden installed the world's first high-definition scoreboard system: four huge screens in the building's main structure and 150 smaller screens scattered elsewhere.

Alphabet Soup

Franklin D. Roosevelt's New Deal created more than 65 government agencies intended to help combat the Great Depression. They quickly became known as "alphabet agencies" because of their handy initialisms. Here are just a few.

Federal Emergency Relief Administration (FERA)

National Recovery Administration (NRA)

Civilian Conservation Corps (CCC)

Public Works Administration (PWA)

Works Progress Administration (WPA)

Federal Deposit Insurance Corporation (FDIC)

Agricultural Adjustment Administration (AAA)

Federal Housing Administration (FHA)

Securities and Exchange Commission (SEC)

National Labor Relations Board (NLRB)

Farm Security Administration (FSA)

Social Security Administration (SSA)

Drought Relief Service (DRS)

Puerto Rico Reconstruction Administration (PRRA)

Farm Credit Administration (FCA)

US ARMY UNITS

SQUAD: 8–12 soldiers

PLATOON: 15–30

COMPANY: 80–150

BATTALION: 300–800

REGIMENT/BRIGADE: 2,000–4,000

DIVISION/LEGION: 10,000–15,000

CORPS: 20,000–40,000

DID YOU KNOW?

"Republican" and "Democrat" are both towns in North Carolina.

FALL OF A GIANT

Sears was once America's largest retailer, but few people born after the 1990s even recognize the brand today. Sears's retail troubles go back to 1993. That was the year the company ended production of its famous "Wish Book"—the phone book–sized catalog that was a staple of American homes, especially at the holidays. It was also the year the company laid off 50,000 employees in an attempt to stave off competition from companies like Walmart. It didn't work. In 2004, Sears underwent a merger with Kmart, which had filed for bankruptcy two years prior to the purchase. Since 2006, Sears has gone from more than 3,000 stores to just 20.

Naming Wrongs

As president, Ronald Reagan preached smaller government and less spending. So why not name one of the biggest and most expensive projects in government history after him? The Ronald Reagan Building and International Trade Center opened in Washington, DC, in 1998, and at 3.1 million square feet, it's the second-largest federal building in the nation. (The largest is the Pentagon, located in Virginia.) And at the time, the Ronald Reagan Building boasted the heftiest price tag for a single structure in U.S. government history: $768 million. (Another ironic naming fact: In 1981, the nation's air-traffic controllers went on strike—and President Reagan fired them all. In 1998, National Airport in Washington was renamed . . . Ronald Reagan National Airport.)

REGIONAL TREAT

SCRAPPLE

FOUND IN: Philadelphia and Delaware

DESCRIPTION: Created by German butchers, scrapple is believed to the be first pork dish that originated in the United States. The main ingredient is pork bits left over from butchering, including the head, liver, and heart. The meat is boiled off the bone, chopped, and added to cornmeal mush along with spices. It's then gelled into loaves, cut into slices, and pan-fried, and served for breakfast, topped with maple syrup.

AMERICA: HOME OF THE WORLD'S LARGEST ...

BALL OF STAMPS

LOCATION: Omaha, Nebraska

DETAILS: Outside of Omaha is Boys Town, the 900-acre orphanage immortalized in the 1938 Spencer Tracy movie of the same name. Boys Town has a stamp museum, which is where visitors can find the Ball. It measures only 32 inches in diameter, but it weighs a whopping 600 pounds, and consists of approximately 4.65 million postage stamps. The Boys Town Stamp Collecting Club started the project in 1953 by sticking stamps onto a golf ball. Just two years later, the ball had reached its current size. Visitors may touch the ball, as long as they don't remove—or add—any stamps. (No word on why the residents of Boys Town ever started the stamp ball in the first place . . .)

That Would Be a Congressional Record

The United States Constitution provides that the House of Representatives have no more than one representative for every 30,000 persons, with a minimum of one per state. The idea behind this number was to keep the House of Representatives close to the people. The numbers of elected representatives in the House continued to grow according to census figures until 1910, by which time there were 435 members. After the 1920 census, there were battles over apportionment; the final result was that Congress voted in 1929 to limit the number of representatives to the existing 435. If the original maximum ratio of one representative per 30,000 people still applied, a small city would have to be built on Capitol Hill to hold them all. After the 2020 census, there would have been 1,048 members of the House. Imagine trying to get anything done with a crowd that big!

A Bargain at Any Price

Until 1917, the US Virgin Islands were owned by Denmark. During World War I, the US government feared that Germany would use the islands for U-boat bases and bought the islands from Denmark for $25 million, the highest price the United States had ever paid for land. The US took possession of the islands in 1917 and granted citizenship to all residents 10 years later.

A CITY OF SUPERLATIVES, PART II

The Big Apple isn't the only big-city nickname. For instance, there's...

CHICAGO, THE CITY OF BIG SHOULDERS: You may know it as the "Windy City" (which refers to blustery politicians, not the weather), but it's also called the "City of Big Shoulders," taken from a line in Carl Sandburg's 1916 poem "Chicago."

SEATTLE, THE EMERALD CITY: This was the winning entry in a 1982 contest held by the Seattle–King County Convention and Visitors Bureau.

POLITICIANS

SPEAK

About the time we think
we can make ends meet,
somebody moves the ends.

—HERBERT HOOVER

IT'S A GRAND OL' TREE

Although it may be low on the Christmas radar for most of us, the massive General Grant Tree, located in California's Kings Canyon National Park, has been America's official Christmas tree for nearly 100 years.

When Charles Lee of Sanger, California, visited the mammoth tree in the mid-1920s, he overheard a little girl say, "What a wonderful Christmas tree it would be." Liking the idea, Lee wrote to the president of the United States about it. Calvin Coolidge designated it the nation's Christmas tree in 1926. Since then, a small group of hardy hikers have made their way to the tree each year for an annual Trek to the Tree celebration. That celebration includes Christmas music and speeches, and a large wreath is placed at the base of the tree.

The General Grant Tree serves a dual purpose as both the national Christmas tree and the only living national shrine dedicated to the memory of soldiers who have died in any US war (a distinction it received in 1956).

IRONY AT WORK

New York City isn't just the most populous city in the United States, it's also a major travel destination, and the area employs an army of restaurant, service, hotel, and hospitality workers. When the COVID-19 pandemic led to stay-at-home orders and government-ordered temporary closures of thousands of "nonessential" businesses in 2020, many of those workers were left unemployed. There was at least one industry that grew, however. New York City's had so many jobless benefit claims that the government's unemployment division had to hire dozens of processors.

DID YOU KNOW?

Of the 48 contiguous United States, 21 border an ocean or gulf.

When Harry Met Bessie

More stories of how our presidents and First Ladies met.

WHEN GRACIE MET CALVIN

One day in 1903, Grace Anna Goodhue was watering flowers outside the Clarke School for the Deaf in Northampton, Massachusetts, where she taught. At some point, she looked up and saw a man through the open window of a boardinghouse across the street. He was shaving, his face covered with lather, and dressed in his long johns. He was also wearing a hat. Grace burst out laughing, and the man turned to look at her. That was the first encounter between Grace and Calvin Coolidge. They were married two years later.

WHEN HARRY MET BESSIE

In 1890, when they were both small children, Harry Truman met Bess Wallace at the Baptist Church in Independence, Missouri. They were both attending Sunday school—he was six, she

was five. Truman later wrote of their first meeting: "We made a number of new acquaintances, and I became interested in one in particular. She had golden curls and has, to this day, the most beautiful blue eyes. We went to Sunday school, public school from the fifth grade through high school, graduated in the same class, and marched down life's road together. For me she still has the blue eyes and golden hair of yesteryear." Bess and Harry were married in 1919.

MEET ME IN COUPON

Real town names in Pennsylvania.

BIRD-IN-HAND

BURNT CABINS

EIGHTY FOUR

FORTY FORT

GLEN CAMPBELL

INTERCOURSE

NANTY-GLO

PANIC

SCALP LEVEL

WILKES-BARRE

Political Entertainers

*Some people just can't get enough of fame,
and the world offers no better stages than entertainment
and politics. Here are some celebrities who became
prominent political figures.*

CLINT EASTWOOD: Actor with attitude turned mayor of Carmel-by-the-Sea, California (1986–88).

FREDERICK L. GRANDY: Lovable *Love Boat* Gopher turned Iowa congressman (1987–94).

BEN JONES: Greasy *Dukes of Hazzard* mechanic turned Georgia congressman (1989–92).

AL FRANKEN: *Saturday Night Live* funnyman turned Minnesota senator (2009–18).

JESSE "THE BODY" VENTURA: Pro wrestler turned Minnesota governor (1999–2003).

SONNY BONO: Cher's hubby turned mayor of Palm Springs (1988–92) turned California congressman (1995–98).

SHIRLEY TEMPLE BLACK: Precocious child star turned delegate to the United Nations (1969–70), turned US ambassador to Ghana (1974–76) and Czechoslovakia (1989–92).

ARNOLD SCHWARZENEGGER: Bodybuilder who won Mr. Universe five times and Mr. Olympia six years in a row (1970–75) turned actor turned California governor (2003–11).

RONALD REAGAN: Actor turned California governor (1967–75) turned 40th US president (1981–89).

And a politician who became a celebrity . . .

JERRY SPRINGER: Cincinnati, Ohio, mayor (1977–78), who, after a failed bid for governor, turned daytime talk-show host.

Join the Flock

The United States' post–World War II housing boom and the rapid growth of suburbia meant that millions of Americans suddenly had homes with front lawns. A company called Union Products of Leominster, Massachusetts, catered to these homeowners, offering dozens of plastic sculptures of animals and cute characters that they called "lawn ornaments." In 1957, Union hired a 19-year-old art school graduate named Don Featherstone to design and create prototypes for even more. His first plastic sculptures for Union Products included a duck that sold so well that he was asked to design another bird, but something more exotic: a flamingo. (Why a flamingo? Union found that its pink products were selling particularly well, and flamingos are pink.) Featherstone couldn't find any live flamingos to use as models (as he'd done with ducks), so he based his design on pictures in *National Geographic*. One deviation from nature: Featherstone made the legs thinner and rod-like, so they could be used to stick the finished plastic version into the ground. The first pink flamingos went on sale in 1958 and cost $2.76 for a pair. It's estimated that 20 million of the birds have been sold since then.

STRANGE PLACES TO SPEND THE NIGHT
Haunted Lighthouse

LOCATION: Atop Lake Superior's rocky cliffs in Michigan's Upper Peninsula

DETAILS: We're not talking a "haunted" lighthouse—true believers truly believe that spirits reside at the Big Bay Point Lighthouse. Built in 1896, this brick home and adjoining lighthouse is one of the few "resident lights" that serves as a bed-and-breakfast. It's estimated that one-fifth of Michigan's 120 lighthouses (the most of any state) are haunted, none more so than Big Bay.

At least five ghosts are said to live there; the most famous is H. William Prior, Big Bay's first keeper. Overtaken with grief after his son died in an accident, Prior hanged himself on the grounds. Guests can enjoy fun activities like hiking the nature trails, gathering around the fireplace, watching the sunset from the lantern, or running out of their rooms in the middle of the night because the dresser drawers keep opening and slamming shut.

The Cash Is in the Mail

Did you receive a piece of junk mail in the spring of 2008, addressed to "Resident" and labeled "National Household Travel Survey"? Don't remember? Then you probably threw it away, as did thousands of others who received the mailer from the Department of Transportation requesting that you take part in a survey about your travel habits. If you'd opened the mailer, you would've found a crisp $5 bill inside (a "token of appreciation"). Had the DOT sent out checks for $5, they could have tracked how many people cashed them and canceled all the checks that weren't cashed. But because they sent out cash, there was no way to trace how many people got the money . . . or how many $5 bills ended up in the trash.

DID YOU KNOW?

It would take 280 million toy army men placed side by side to completely surround the perimeter of the contiguous United States.

Honk if You Voted

*Americans practice their First Amendment rights
on their cars' rear bumpers.*

MY KID IS AN HONOR STUDENT
AND MY PRESIDENT IS AN IDIOT

**BE NICE TO AMERICA OR WE'LL BRING
DEMOCRACY TO YOUR COUNTRY**

There Are a Lot of Pros and Cons in Politics

You Can't Fix Stupid,
But You Can Vote It Out

**DON'T STEAL.
THE GOVERNMENT HATES COMPETITION**

Visualize Impeachment

At Least the War on the Middle Class is Going Well

A Woman's Place is in the House . . . and Senate

SMILE! YOU'RE ON HOMELAND SECURITY CAMERA!

Politicians and Diapers Need to Be Changed . . .
Often for the Same Reason

All Politics Is Loco

GERM WARFARE

In an average day, the president of the United States meets—and shakes hands with—175 people. That's about 65,000 people a year . . . and 65,000 people's germs. Many politicians have no choice but to use hand sanitizer as frequently as possible. Former president George W. Bush reportedly went through a bottle a week; he even applied some immediately after shaking incoming president Barack Obama's hand for the first time. Obama was put off, but not too long into his presidency, he began including in his entourage a staffer who dispensed the Purell.

American Wit

We may not imagine
how our lives could be
more frustrating and complex,
but Congress can.

—CULLEN HIGHTOWER

OWNED BY BUFFETT

Through his holding company, Berkshire Hathaway, famous businessman and investor Warren Buffett has amassed a fortune worth over $110 billion, making him one of the wealthiest Americans. Buffett believes in diversification; here are just some of the companies controlled by the "the Oracle of Omaha."

HELZBERG DIAMONDS

SEE'S CANDIES

DAIRY QUEEN

THE PAMPERED CHEF

ORIENTAL TRADING COMPANY

FRUIT OF THE LOOM

BENJAMIN MOORE & CO.

FOREST RIVER

GEICO AUTO INSURANCE

KRAFT HEINZ

DURACELL

FIVE FREAKY FACTS ABOUT ...
THE STATUE OF LIBERTY

- The statue's outer copper coating is just 0.09" thick—thinner than two pennies.

- Lady Liberty's green color is the result of patina, or tarnish on the copper.

- She has a Morton's toe. Named for orthopedist Dudley J. Morton, it's a condition in which the second toe is longer than the big toe, and it affects about 20 percent of people. Long before Dr. Morton, the condition was known as Grecian foot—because in classical and Renaissance art, a long second toe was considered beautiful. Lady Liberty's sculptor was inspired by the statues of the ancient Greeks and Romans, including this classic feature of ancient Greek art.

- In November 1886, the statue became the nation's first electric lighthouse when nine electric arc lamps were installed in her torch, and five placed around her base. The torch, at 305 feet above sea level, was visible 24 miles out to sea and acted as a navigational light until 1902.

- She's just over 111 feet tall, her face is ten feet wide, and her feet are 25 feet long—which means she wears a size 879 sandal.

SEAL the Deal

Elite US Navy SEALs (Sea, Air, and Land Forces) comprise less than 1 percent of navy personnel. Ever dream of joining this exclusive group? To qualify for the training program, you must pass an initial physical screening that includes:

* ★ 500-yard swim using breast- or sidestroke in 12:30 (under 10:00 to be competitive)

* ★ 42 push-ups in 2 minutes (100 to be competitive)

* ★ 50 sit-ups in 2 minutes (100 to be competitive)

* ★ 6 pull-ups, no time limit (15 to be competitive)

* ★ 1.5-mile run in boots and trousers in 11:30 (under 10:20 to be competitive)

And if you get in, training will consist of:

* ★ 8 weeks at the Special Warfare Preparatory School

* ★ 3 weeks at the Indoctrination Course

* ★ 24 weeks of Basic Underwater Demolition/SEAL training (physical conditioning, diving, and land warfare), including "Hell Week," 132 hours of continuous physical activity. A typical class loses 70–80 percent of its trainees in this phase.

* ★ 15 weeks of SEAL Qualification Training (learning special skills and tactics, as well as developing the ability to lead others), including 4 weeks of cold-weather training. Those left standing are awarded the SEAL trident and assigned to a team . . . then there's *more* training!

AMERICA: HOME OF THE WORLD'S LARGEST . . .
Light Bulb

LOCATION: Edison, New Jersey

DETAILS: A 13-foot, eight-ton incandescent light bulb tops the Edison Memorial Tower at the Thomas Edison Center. The giant bulb was installed in 1937, made up of 153 individual pieces of amber-colored Corning Pyrex glass, each two inches thick. And the bulb actually still works, lighting up the neighborhood nightly. The concrete tower (and the big bulb) stand on the exact spot where Edison developed his original (much, much smaller) light bulb in 1879.

The Corn Dog

ORIGINS OF AMERICA'S FAVORITE PORTABLE SNACK.
Take a hot dog, impale it on a stick, cover that sucker
with cornmeal, and what have you got? The beginning of
a battle, that's what. On one side is the Texas State Fair,
which says the corny dog (corn dog to some) was invented
by a couple of vaudevillians, Neil and Carl Fletcher of
Dallas, who sold them from a fair booth in 1942. The
other contender is Springfield, Illinois, which tried to
convince the world it's the site of the first dog of a corny
nature. Unfortunately for Illinois, their dogs' origin story
traces back to Texas . . .

Ed Waldmire Jr. claims he saw a strange sandwich in
Oklahoma consisting of a wiener baked in cornbread.
When his friend came up with a mix that would stick to
a wiener so it could be deep-fried, Ed put a stick in it and
called it Crusty Cur. At his wife's urging, he changed the
name to Cozy Dog and eventually sold it in a Springfield
restaurant of the same name. Thing is . . . the actual
inventing took place while Ed was stationed at an air force
base in Amarillo. So either way, Texas can claim credit for
the corn dog.

PRESIDENTIAL PENSION

These days, outgoing presidents are almost guaranteed a lucrative publishing deal to write their memoirs. When Harry Truman left office in 1953, he was offered several commercial endorsements and corporate positions, but turned them all down, believing them to be inappropriate for a former president. Instead, Truman retired on his US Army pension of $112.56 a month. It wasn't enough, though. There was no retirement package for ex-presidents, so Truman had to take out a bank loan to get by. By the mid-1950s, faced with financial ruin, Truman changed his mind and signed a deal to write his memoirs, which included an account of his White House years—something only a few previous US presidents had ever done. (In 1958, Congress passed the Former Presidents Act, which gave a lifetime pension to former presidents.)

Tip of the Ice Cube

In the aftermath of Hurricane Katrina in 2005, the Federal Emergency Management Agency (FEMA) purchased 112,000 tons of ice for $24 million. Unfortunately, they were unable to distribute all of it to those in need, so they stored the unused ice in cold warehouses. Two years later, the ice was still in storage—and the cost to keep it cold all that time totaled more than $11 million, nearly half of what it cost to purchase. Even more embarrassing, it was announced that because FEMA didn't know the "shelf life" for ice, the stockpile couldn't be reused and had to be melted. The cost of the melting operation: another $3.4 million. (FEMA subsequently announced that they are no longer in the business of buying and storing ice for disasters.)

NOWHERE NEAR DENVER

The Denver omelet, an American diner classic, is made with eggs, ham, cheese, diced green peppers, and diced onions. Restaurants in Denver may have appropriated it, but the dish started as a version of the Chinese dish egg foo yong, introduced to the United States by Chinese railroad workers in the late 1800s. That entrée consists of eggs, ham, and whatever vegetables are available. Workers ate it on bread to make it more portable, and American cooks later adapted it into an omelet (with toast on the side).

DID YOU KNOW?

A lawsuit is filed in the US every 30 seconds.

PARANORMAL PARKS,
PART II

America's national parks are full of ghostly tales...

PLANE CRASH VICTIMS: GRAND CANYON NATIONAL PARK, ARIZONA

In 1956, two planes collided over the Grand Canyon and crashed into the cliffs. Both were flying off course—flight experts believe the pilots were trying to give their passengers better views. More than 120 people died, and the site was so remote that rescue and clean-up crews couldn't reach some of the debris or bodies, so they remained in an area that park rangers later called Crash Canyon.

Almost 50 years later, ranger K. J. Glover was camping at the floor of Crash Canyon and awoke in the middle of the night to confused voices and footsteps outside her tent. She peeked out to see a group of people passing by her campsite. The men and women were dressed up in fashions that weren't modern, and certainly weren't appropriate for a midnight hike. Glover watched as the group passed her and continued up the canyon toward the site of the 1956 crash. In the morning, Glover realized she could have been dreaming, but she believed she'd been fully awake and seeing the ghosts of the people who died in those plane crashes five decades earlier.

THE FRENCH QUARTER 15 DOZEN CLUB

Acme Oyster House in New Orleans has an exclusive club: its members have met the challenge of slurping down 15 dozen oysters—that's 180 raw oysters—in an hour. Entrants must sign a medical release form before starting the meal, but are allowed breaks (which are supervised to ensure no purging takes place). If you finish the challenge, your name is added to the coveted 15 Dozen Board, and you'll walk away with a free hat and T-shirt. Your bill will also be cut in half—or canceled altogether, if you beat the house record. But that's no small feat: the current leader is Brad Sciullo of Uniontown, Pennsylvania, with 43 dozen. (That's *516 raw oysters.*)

DID YOU KNOW?

The eyes have it: 45 percent of Americans have brown eyes, 27 percent have blue, and 9 percent have green.

A REVOLUTIONARY BAR TAB

The delegates at the American Constitutional Convention had more than the country's well-being in mind when they were preparing the Constitution. A party bill from Philadelphia's City Tavern from two days before the official signing shows the gentlemen—only 55 of them, mind you—made quick work of 156 bottles of liquor, including 60 bottles of claret and eight bottles of whiskey, along with seven bowls of Alcoholic Punch. The bill—which also included dinner, music, and fees for broken glasses—came out to a little over £89, or about $15,500 in today's money. Cheers!

FAST-FOOD FOUNDERS
A&W Root Beer

NOW: A&W is one of the world's best-selling root beers, and there are nearly 1,000 A&W fast-food restaurants in North America.

THEN: On a hot June day in 1919, during a World War I veterans' parade, Roy Allen opened a root beer stand in Lodi, California. Allen charged just a nickel a serving, and so many people loved his root beer that he opened another stand in Sacramento. Business continued to grow, and in 1922, he brought in a partner, Frank Wright. The men combined their initials and A&W Root Beer was born.

Much of their success came from the drinks and hamburgers they sold, but they were also shrewd businessmen who took advantage of Prohibition. Allen and Wright sold their root "beer" in large frosty mugs and decorated their restaurants to look like saloons. Many drinkers seemed to enjoy the ambience even without the alcohol. A&W was also one of the first hamburger joints to offer drive-up carhop service. In 1924, Allen bought out Wright and started selling franchises so that people could open their own A&Ws, a move that turned the small collection of California eateries into one of the first nationally successful restaurant chains.

POLITICIANS
SPEAK

I believe in an America where
millions of Americans believe in an
America that's the America millions
of Americans believe in.
That's the America I love!

—MITT ROMNEY

ALIEN ABDUCTION INSURANCE

Which is stranger—that a Florida company sells alien abduction insurance policies? Or that one of the claims was actually paid? The $10 million policy, created in 1987 by Mike St. Lawrence, costs $29.95 and covers "outpatient psychiatric care" as well as the "sarcasm factor" the abductee may incur from doubting family members. You can't be turned down due to age or "frequent flyer

status." One other important detail: the policy is a joke. The legalese concludes with, "If you don't get it . . . you can't get it."

But that hasn't stopped some people from taking it seriously. St. Lawrence estimated in 2019 that, of the 6,000 alien abduction policies his company has sold, about half the buyers are true believers. That being said, proof of abduction is required for a payout. That payout was actually made to a claimant who told St. Lawrence that he showed an "implanted alien chip" to an MIT professor, who determined the chip was "not of this earth." As the policy states, the $10 million payout will be paid in annual installments of $1 for the next ten million years.

(If aliens aren't your concern, you can also purchase reincarnation insurance that you can collect on in your next life—pursuant to proof that you were, in fact, reincarnated.)

DID YOU KNOW?

State with the most UFO sightings per capita: Washington.

JFK'S Eagles

In 1985, Norman Braman, owner of the NFL's Philadelphia Eagles, was visiting the US Capitol when Senator Ted Kennedy told him the story of how his brother John F. Kennedy had considered buying the Eagles in October 1962. Not yet two years into his first term as president, JFK was already thinking about what he would do after leaving office. When he learned the Eagles were for sale, he and their other brother Bobby instructed Ted to go to Philadelphia to meet with the team's management and discuss a possible sale. But Ted never went, and someone else bought the Eagles. "What happened?" Braman asked. "The Cuban Missile Crisis," Ted told him.

FIRST "FIRST LADY"

Lacy Ware Webb Hayes, wife of Rutherford B. Hayes, was the first First Lady to be *called* First Lady. From Martha Washington through Julie Grant, presidential wives did not have a title. In 1876, newspaper writer Mary Clemmer Ames first referred to Mrs. Hayes, wife of the 19th president, as "the First Lady" in her column "Woman's Letter from Washington."

THE HUGHES H-1

In 1934, eccentric millionaire aviator Howard Hughes built an experimental plane called the H-1. In January 1937, it set a transcontinental speed record by flying at 332 mph from California to New Jersey, making it the fastest plane in the world. Hughes proposed to the US Army that they base a fighter plane on the design, but they weren't interested. Japan was. Mitsubishi engineer Jiro Horikoshi designed a fighter plane that incorporated many of the H-1's features: the "Zero" was the premier fighter plane of World War II. The United States and its allies didn't develop a plane that could match it until 1943.

Oval Office Origins

The Oval Office is such a symbol of the American presidency that it's hard to imagine a time when the commander-in-chief didn't reside there. Prior to Theodore Roosevelt, office space was primarily found in the White House's second floor. But it wasn't long after Roosevelt moved in, in 1901, that he realized the building wouldn't be big enough for both his large family and his presidential staff. So he ordered the construction of a West Wing that would serve as office space for himself and his administration, freeing up some second-floor offices in the Executive Mansion to be converted into more living space for the First Family. But Roosevelt's West Wing office was rectangular. It wasn't until his successor, William Howard Taft, doubled the size of the West Wing in 1909, that a new, oval-shaped office was added to serve as the president's work space.

Though Teddy never occupied the Oval Office, his desk did. When Taft moved into the newly completed office in October 1909, he continued to use the "Roosevelt desk" he'd inherited from his predecessor: a sturdy but plain mahogany desk built in the Federalist style that he set in front of the large windows that faced south.

On Broadway

Or off Broadway? What's the difference, anyway?

Writing, producing, or starring in a Broadway play is considered the peak of success for many in the entertainment business, and attending one is a rite of passage for many Americans moving to or visiting New York City. Most of the Broadway theaters happen to be in the city's main theater district in Times Square, through which Broadway Avenue runs. But does that mean every performance there is "on Broadway"?

★ A show being deemed a "Broadway play" does not necessarily mean that it's being produced at a theater on Broadway itself. Instead, it indicates the size of the theater. Broadway venues are the ones with the most seats: 500 or more. Off-Broadway theaters have 100 to 499 seats; off-off-Broadway, fewer than 100.

★ The Vivian Beaumont Theater is the one Broadway theater not in Times Square: it's located at Lincoln Center.

★ Only five theaters have a Broadway address. The rest are in the West 40s and 50s.

Break a leg!

Continuing Adventures of Florida Man

HAMBURGLAR

In December 2017, a Florida Man named Maeli Aguilar-Alvarez, 26, was walking out of an Indiantown convenience store, trying to look as innocent as possible. But a sheriff's sergeant sitting in a nearby squad car noticed something suspicious about the way Aguilar-Alvarez was walking and asked if he happened to have anything stuffed down his pants. Then the cop noticed a strong smell of alcohol, and a search commenced. Aguilar-Alvarez removed a full rack of ribs from his pants . . . and that was just the beginning. According to *TCPalm*, "A further search yielded two packs of hamburger buns, nine pieces of fried chicken, and some mashed potatoes."

Taco Liberty Bell

Americans are used to corporate sponsorships, but we have to put our foot down somewhere!

In 1996, Taco Bell took out an ad in the *New York Times* and announced that the company had recently purchased the Liberty Bell (on display at Philadelphia's National Historic Park). The company compared the purchase to the popular "adopt-a-road"

programs in the United States in which companies sponsor a highway and finance its upkeep. In the ad, Taco Bell wrote, "We hope our move will prompt other corporations to take similar action to do their part to reduce the country's debt."

The National Historic Park offices were flooded with calls from angry citizens protesting the park service's decision to sell off the Liberty Bell—a national treasure!—to a corporation. But (thankfully) it was all a hoax: the ad ran on April Fool's Day and was, said Taco Bell in a later press release, "the best joke of the day."

It wasn't the only joke of the day, however. Also on April 1, 1996, Bill Clinton's White House spokesperson, Mike McCurry, announced that the government planned to sell the Lincoln Memorial to Ford, who intended to change the memorial's name to the "Lincoln-Mercury Memorial." April Fool's!

AMERICA: HOME OF THE WORLD'S LARGEST ... ROTATING GLOBE

LOCATION: Yarmouth, Maine

DETAILS: David DeLorme, Chairman and CEO of DeLorme, a mapping-software company, commissioned the globe for his company headquarters in 1996. At 41 feet across and three stories tall, "Eartha" is the largest reproduction of the Earth ever constructed. Visitors to DeLorme can view Eartha at three different levels: North Pole, South Pole, and the equator. The globe spins on its axis at a 23.5-degree angle, just like the real Earth, and is covered in 792 computer-generated map panels. It makes one complete revolution (representing a day) in 18 minutes.

American Wit

Tip the world over on its side
and everything loose
will land in Los Angeles.

—FRANK LLOYD WRIGHT

STRANGER LAWS

★ In Providence, Rhode Island, it's illegal to sell toothbrushes on Sundays. (Toothpaste is OK.)

★ It's against the law in Washington state to pretend that your parents are rich.

★ Women in Corvallis, Oregon, are not legally permitted to drink coffee after 6:00 p.m.

★ By law, Washington drivers must carry an anchor to be used as an emergency brake.

PREFERRED PLEDGE POSITION

The Pledge of Allegiance was originally drafted in 1892, by former Baptist minister Francis Bellamy. It's been through several changes over the years, and one of the most important occurred in 1942. What was known until then as the "Bellamy Salute" had been pledged by Americans with their arms outstretched toward the flag, palms facing down. Sound familiar? It was also the same salute the Nazi Party was using in Germany. So, just like it was with the US national anthem, the gesture was changed to placing the right hand over the heart.

DID YOU KNOW?

Official state language of Illinois between 1923 and 1969: "American."

MICKEY'S BFF

It's obvious where Donald Duck's surname came from (he's a duck), but what about "Donald"? The most likely theory: When Walt Disney was creating Mickey Mouse's best friend in 1932, he read about Donald Bradman in the papers. The Australian cricketing legend, while on a North American goodwill tour in 1932, scored what's called a duck (similar to a strikeout in baseball). A popular editorial cartoon featured a somewhat familiar-looking duck wearing a shirt that says "Donald's Duck." Not long after, Disney's Donald Duck debuted.

Donald isn't the only member of the Duck family. Throughout the character's long history, Disney writers have worked out an extensive family tree for him. Among Donald's relatives: his sister Delia (mother of Huey, Dewey, and Louie), Gladstone Gander, Abner "Whitewater" Duck, Gus Goose, Downy O'Drake (Scrooge McDuck's father), Fanny Coot, Molly Mallard, "Dirty" Dingus McDuck, Gretchen Grebe, and Gertrude Gadwall.

THE PEANUT GALLERY

Americans have botanist and chemist George Washington Carver (1861–1943) to thank for one of our favorite snack foods: peanut butter. But if you're hankering for a peanut snack besides butter, you're in luck: Carver developed more than 300 different products from peanuts—including . . . Breakfast Food (five different kinds), Peanut Surprise, Malted Peanuts, Bisque Powder, Peanut Meal (brown), Chili Sauce, Dry Coffee, Cream Candy, Instant Coffee, Peanut Hearts, Chop Suey Sauce, Mock Oysters, Mayonnaise, Worcestershire Sauce, Peanut Meat Loaf, Peanut Sprouts, Peanut Tofu Sauce, Buttermilk, Mock Meat, Mock Goose, Mock Duck, Mock Chicken, Mock Veal Cut, Curds, Vinegar, Crystallized Peanuts, Peanut Relish, Peanut Sausage, Sweet Pickle, Substitute Asparagus, and Mock Coconut, along with Toilet Soap, Fuel Bricketts, Printers Ink, Rubber, and Gasoline.

LITTLE SURE SHOT

Annie Oakley was an icon of the Wild West—she spent years touring with Buffalo Bill Cody's Wild West Show. But her name wasn't Annie, and she wasn't from the West. Oakley was born Phoebe Ann Mosely in 1860, in Darke County, Ohio. "Annie" came from young Phoebe's middle name, but "Oakley" comes from the Cincinnati suburb of Oakley, near where she and her husband (fellow sharpshooter Frank Butler) lived during the early years of their marriage. (Another name she used: Watanya Cicilla, meaning "Little Sure Shot," given to her by her friend and fellow Wild West Show participant Chief Sitting Bull.)

Ben Franklin's Veggies

Long before people figured out that eating citrus fruit could prevent diseases like scurvy, Benjamin Franklin was touting the advantages of daily servings of fruit. "An apple a day keeps the doctor away" is one of his most famous sayings, but Franklin also claimed that oranges, limes, and grapefruit were healthy, especially for the gums and skin. He also advocated a vegetarian diet, believing that it "promoted clearness of ideas and quickness of thought." He was fine with eating fish, though—he reasoned that, since fish sometimes ate one another, it was acceptable for humans to eat fish, too.

Constitution Rejects

In order to form a more perfect union, delegates to the 1787 Constitutional Convention tossed these suggestions into history's circular file.

THREE PRESIDENTS. Delegates led by Elbridge Gerry of Massachusetts feared a single president would become too kinglike, and proposed a committee of three—one from the northern states, one from the middle, and one from the southern.

A PRESIDENT FOR LIFE. Alexander Hamilton wanted a president who would serve indefinitely so long as he exhibited "good behavior," otherwise ex-presidents would end up wandering the country "like ghosts" pining for their former glory, stirring up trouble.

PRESIDENT AS SECRETARY. Roger Sherman of Connecticut suggested that the president be little more than a clerk, a simple administrator to make sure laws passed by Congress were implemented.

ELIMINATION OF STATES. George Read of Delaware called for the erasure of state boundaries and elimination of state governments. In the spirit of compromise, Benjamin Franklin—president of the Pennsylvania Executive Council—generously offered to deed large chunks of his state to New Jersey and Delaware.

VETO POWER. James Madison thought Congress should have the power to veto laws passed by state legislatures. (He also wanted Congress to set up a national university.)

PRESIDENTS WHO SERVED

US ARMY/NATIONAL GUARD: George Washington, Thomas Jefferson (Virginia militia), James Madison (Virginia militia), James Monroe (Virginia militia), Andrew Jackson, William Henry Harrison, John Tyler (Virginia militia), James K. Polk (Tennessee militia), Zachary Taylor, Millard Fillmore (New York militia), Franklin Pierce, James Buchanan (Pennsylvania militia), Abraham Lincoln (Illinois militia), Andrew Johnson, Ulysses S. Grant, Rutherford B. Hayes, James Garfield, Chester A. Arthur (New York militia), Benjamin Harrison, William McKinley, Theodore Roosevelt, Harry S. Truman, Dwight D. Eisenhower, and Ronald Reagan

US NAVY: John F. Kennedy, Lyndon B. Johnson, Richard Nixon, Gerald Ford, Jimmy Carter, and George H. W. Bush

US AIR FORCE: George W. Bush, through his time in the Texas Air National Guard

(No presidents have been members of the US Coast Guard or US Marine Corps.)

A Covered Bridge Too Far

New York State is home to many historic covered bridges—old, wooden structures built between 1823 and 1912. Here are some favorites:

* The Hyde Hall Bridge, the oldest surviving covered bridge in the United States, can be found in Gillmerglass State Park in Otsego County. Built in 1923, the bridge spans a small body of water called Shadow Brook on the Hyde Hall country estate, which belonged to George Clarke, son of New York's colonial governor (also named George Clarke).

* The New York State Covered Bridge Society calls the 232-foot long and 26-foot-wide Blenheim Bridge (1855), which crosses Schoharie Creek, the "longest single span wooden bridge in the world."

* Just north of Albany, between the towns of Buskirk and Salem, are three covered bridges that span the Battenkill River. The Eagleville (built in 1858) and Rexleigh (1874) bridges still let vehicles pass, but the Shushan (1858) is for pedestrians only. A sign on the Shushan reads, "Five-dollar fine for riding or driving on this bridge faster than a walk."

REGIONAL TREAT

RUNZA

FOUND IN: Nebraska and Kansas

DESCRIPTION: German and Russian immigrants settled in the region in the late 1800s and developed this dish: a stuffed bread pocket, filled with minced beef, pork, sauerkraut, and onions. If you get one in Nebraska, it will be rectangular. A Kansas runza is usually round.

POLITICIANS

SPEAK

It's a damn poor mind

that can only think

of one way to

spell a word.

—ANDREW JACKSON

FIVE FREAKY FACTS ABOUT ...
FLORIDA

* New Mexico was the nation's "Sunshine State" for nearly 50 years, but that motto was never officially adopted by a government resolution. In 1970, when some envious Floridians became aware of this, Tallahassee lawmakers swooped in and "stole" the Sunshine State motto in broad daylight.

* In 2015, Guinness World Records confirmed that—at 1,277 individual pieces—the South Florida Museum has the world's largest collection of coprolite (more commonly known as fossilized poop).

* Florida has spent more time as a part of Spain (from 1513 to 1819, or 306 years) than as a part of the United States—200 years as of this writing.

* Fifty-three percent of the residents of Sumter County (near Orlando) are at least 65 years old. That makes Sumter the only county in the country where the elderly are the majority.

* America's Australia: not only is Florida the only place alligators and crocodiles coexist, it has six species of venomous snakes; thirteen species of bats; black, red, and brown widows; wild pigs; and the most shark attacks of any state—more than 800 since 1845.

STORMING AREA 51

Area 51—the top-secret US Air Force base in Nevada—is too heavily guarded for a small group of UFO enthusiasts to infiltrate . . . but thousands of true believers could overrun the place. At least, that was the thinking behind "Storm Area 51," a Facebook event scheduled for September 20, 2019. Anyone who wanted to "See Them Aliens" could take part in a Japanese manga-inspired "Naruto run." (That's when you lean forward with your arms extended straight behind you and run as fast as you can.) "We can run faster than their bullets!" wrote Matty Roberts, who posted the event as a joke.

But matters turned much more serious a few weeks before the event when news leaked that some US senators had been briefed about

"encounters between the US Navy and an unidentified aircraft." To Roberts's surprise, and to the locals' dismay, more than 300,000 people clicked that they were "going" to what was being called "Alienstock" in Rachel, Nevada (pop. 54). Two million more were "interested." The Facebook event was removed: event canceled. When the big day arrived, a few thousand people (not including Roberts) showed up to find a formidable police and military presence. Only one person attempted the Naruto run . . . unsuccessfully. There were no reports of aliens, but a Canadian citizen was arrested for indecent exposure.

DID YOU KNOW?

Lesser-known names for Area 51: Dreamland, Paradise Ranch, Groom Lake, and Watertown.

Top 10 Favorite Sandwiches in the US

1. **GRILLED CHEESE**
2. **GRILLED CHICKEN**
3. **TURKEY**
4. **ROAST BEEF**
5. **HAM**
6. **BLT**
7. **CLUB**
8. **BACON**
9. **PEANUT BUTTER AND JELLY**
10. **PULLED PORK**

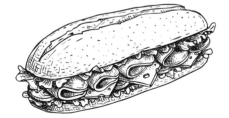

Political Pig

CANDIDATE: Giggles, a nine-month-old pig owned by Michael Ewing, a Flint, Michigan, defense attorney

RUNNING FOR: Mayor of Flint

CAMPAIGN NOTES: Ewing decided to enter Giggles in the 2015 mayoral campaign after election officials publicized the wrong date as the filing deadline for the mayoral primary. The actual filing deadline was earlier than the publicized date, causing every single candidate to miss it—and turning them all into write-in candidates. Ewing thought this made the campaign less transparent, which was a big problem considering that one candidate had served nearly 19 years in prison for murder, and another had been convicted of driving drunk the wrong way down the highway on four flat tires. "Giggles was sitting next to me while I was reading reports about the candidates and I said to her, 'You would make a better candidate than these people.' So I did what any normal person would do—I ran her for mayor," Ewing told the *Huffington Post* in May 2015.

A month later, when state officials passed a special law that allowed the (human) candidates' names to appear on the ballot, Ewing announced that Giggles was pulling out of the race. Which of her opponents did she endorse? None of them, because she was just a pig.

Ben Franklin Pinched My Bum!

When Europeans colonized the New World, a tradition began of burying parishioners on church grounds. As settlements grew into villages, and then to towns and to cities, these churchyards became overrun with dead bodies. In 1719, surveyors in Philadelphia set aside land on the outskirts of town to be made into a massive cemetery that could accommodate thousands of graves. Christ Church Burial Ground became the first cemetery in the future United States. (Now, of course, the outskirts of what was then Old Town is the middle of downtown Philadelphia.)

Christ Church's most famous inhabitant is Benjamin Franklin, best known for signing the Declaration of Independence and inventing things like libraries and bifocals. For Americans today, he is less known for his debauchery—

from bedding his elderly landlady in lieu of paying rent, to engaging in trysts in French dungeons. Death, it would seem, hasn't slowed Franklin down. In 1976, a nurse visiting Christ Church reported that he threw pennies at her, and a handful of other witnesses have claimed that the Founding Father's ghost pinched them on the bottom.

THIS OLD HOUSE

William Winchester—marketer of the Winchester repeating rifle used widely on the Western frontier—died in 1881, leaving his widow, Sarah, with a staggering income of roughly $1,000 per day. But her grief and depression over her husband's death (combined with grief from the loss of her young daughter in 1866) led her to seek guidance from a Boston spiritualist. The Boston medium announced that Sarah's family had died as an act of revenge, undertaken by the ghosts of people killed by Winchester rifles. Maybe because Sarah already felt guilty about those death-dealing rifles, she believed the ghost story. She didn't even argue when the spiritualist told her how to appease the angry spirits: the Winchester widow must move from New Haven, Connecticut, to the West and build a mansion that would never be finished. As long as she kept on building, Sarah would stay alive.

Sarah fled to the farming community of San Jose, California, in 1884. She settled into a small farmhouse, set up a seance room, and each night communicated with "the spirits" who told her what

to build next. The clatter of hammer and saws filled the house 24 hours a day. Sarah employed a legion of builders who worked in shifts for 38 continuous years fulfilling her odd demands. The result: a rambling maze with staircases that led nowhere, over 2,000 cupboards (some only an inch deep), doorways that opened onto nothing, and balconies with no access. Sarah installed five separate central heating systems and strung miles of wire connecting strange communication systems that no one knew how to work. She developed a fixation with the number 13, building rooms with 13 windows each, suites with 13 fireplaces, chandeliers with 13 gaslights, kitchen drains with 13 holes, and more.

Sarah Winchester died in 1922 at age 83, having lived the long life that her spirits supposedly promised her if she kept building. By that time, her mansion—now a museum known as the Winchester Mystery House—boasted 160 rooms, 3 elevators, 6 kitchens, 40 bedrooms, 47 fireplaces, 17 chimneys, 10,000 windows, and 467 doors—but just one shower.

The Tape that Changed History

In the early morning of June 17, 1972, an $80-a-week security guard named Frank Wills was patrolling the parking garage of an office complex in Washington, DC, when he noticed that someone had used adhesive tape to prevent a stairwell door from latching. Wills removed the tape and continued on his rounds, but when he returned to the same door at 2:00 a.m., he saw it had been taped again. So he called the police, who discovered a team of burglars planting bugs in an office leased by the Democratic National Committee. This "third-rate burglary"—and the coverup that followed—grew into the Watergate scandal that forced President Richard M. Nixon to resign from office in 1974.

A Wild Gerrymander

We've all heard the term, used to describe redividing a state or county into election districts that make odd shapes but that give one party a majority. But where did it come from? The word was coined in 1812 when Massachusetts governor Elbridge Gerry redrew Congressional lines in order to give his Democrat-Republican party an advantage over the Federalists. A Boston newspaper ran a political cartoon showing that one of Gerry's new districts looked a lot like a salamander. The word *gerrymandering* was born, and the bad publicity cost Gerry the election.

DINER LINGO

Old-school diner terms you might still hear from behind the counter.

BLOWOUT PATCHES
Pancakes

BUCKET OF COLD MUD
Chocolate ice cream

BURN ONE
To put a hamburger on the grill

HOCKEY PUCK
A well-done hamburger

ON THE HOOF
Meat served rare

PIN A ROSE ON IT
Add an onion

RABBIT FOOD
Lettuce

SINKERS AND SUDS
Doughnuts and coffee

WAX
American cheese

WHISTLEBERRIES
Baked beans

WHITE COW
A vanilla milk shake

WRECK 'EM
Scrambled eggs

Thwarting the Paparazzi

American celebrities are a source of endless entertainment. So are the photographers constantly trying to snap their photo.

TAYLOR SWIFT: In 2017, when Swift was recording her album *Reputation*, paparazzi were camped outside her New York apartment and at her recording studio, but she couldn't be found. Meanwhile, her bodyguards walked to and from her SUV carrying a large suitcase . . . with the 120-pound singer-songwriter curled up inside.

KIM KARDASHIAN: If you're a paparazzo (the singular of paparazzi) and you photograph Kardashian, take a really close look at the images, because there's a good chance you've just photographed a look-alike body double employed by the diva.

LENNY KRAVITZ: After being fed up with the paparazzi profiting by taking pictures of him, Kravitz decided *he* would profit by taking pictures of *them*. The result: *Flash*, a 2015 coffee-table book featuring black-and-white photos of swarms of paparazzi pointing their cameras at the singer.

KATY PERRY: The pop star purchased, as she described it, a "GIANT donut pillow" in New York City before boarding

a flight to Miami. Why? "When getting off the plane, it was the best paparazzi shield."

ALEC BALDWIN: Is that a ghost walking down Hollywood Boulevard? No, it's Alec Baldwin with a sheet covering his entire body, trying (unsuccessfully) not to draw attention to himself. (Another method Baldwin has used to thwart the paparazzi: punch them.)

DUSTIN HOFFMAN: Do yourself a favor and do an image search for "Dustin Hoffman hides from paparazzi." Whenever he sees a lens pointed his way, he hides . . . but not all the way. Hoffman will slowly peek out from behind a wall, a parking meter, a shrub, a tree branch, a book called *The Best Things to Do in Los Angeles* . . .

Bob Hope and the USO

*Legendary entertainer Bob Hope was
as well-known for supporting US troops through
the United Service Organizations—or the USO—as he
was for his acting, singing, and dancing.*

★ He went to Vietnam nine times.

★ He entertained for the USO every year from
1942 to 1990.

★ He headlined approximately 60 tours.

★ The first Bob Hope Christmas Tour was in
1943; he visited military bases each December
for the next 34 years.

★ He started carrying his trademark golf club
during his 1969 USO tour.

★ He became the "first and only honorary
veteran of the US armed forces" by a 1997 act
of Congress signed by President Bill Clinton.

BUMPASS WHAT

Bumpass Hell—a unique hydrothermal hiking area within Mt. Lassen Volcanic National Park, in Shasta County, California—is named for early settler Kendall Vanhook Bumpass. In 1864, he stumbled upon the site, which was filled with fumaroles (holes through which hot gases are released) and boiling pools of water. He described the steamy area as "hell" to a reporter, and for Bumpass it really was: while showing his discovery to the press, he stepped onto a thin crust of ground covering a boiling pool. He burned his leg so badly that it had to be amputated.

OUCH!

About 750 Americans lose a finger in snowblower accidents each year.

IT'S ALSO A CONSPIRACY!

Americans actually believed this, too?
Yep!

THEORY: Reggae superstar Bob Marley was a voice for political change in Jamaica. But when he opposed the puppet government in place there, he was murdered . . . by George H. W. Bush's son Neil Bush.

THE STORY: In 1980, the US-backed International Monetary Fund (IMF) was offering loans to developing nations. Jamaican president Michael Manley turned the IMF down because he thought it would make him a puppet of American business interests and the CIA. The CIA was furious, so it worked with American-born Jamaican politician Edward Seaga to force Manley out of office. But an outspoken critic of the IMF plan was Jamaica's other most influential voice: Bob Marley. One night as Marley slept, two of Seaga's goons went to the singer's home in Kingston and shot him. But Marley didn't die—he went to a mountain retreat to recuperate, where he was interviewed by a reporter from *Rolling Stone*. When Marley's manager called the magazine a few days later, editors told him they hadn't sent a reporter.

So who had been there? Neil Bush, CIA operative and son of former CIA director George H. W. Bush. While Marley was asleep, Bush injected him with a syringe of "something," and a few months later, in May 1981, Marley died at age 36 of cancer.

THE TRUTH: Manley rejected the IMF loan, but he wasn't overthrown—his party simply lost power in 1980. As for Bob Marley, he was diagnosed with cancer far earlier, in 1977, and died four years later. He was never shot and never went to a mountain retreat, so he never had a chance to "get" cancer from Neil Bush.

A Berry Good Side Dish

Canned or fresh? Or both? It's an age-old dilemma—
but whatever your preference, the holidays aren't
the holidays without cranberry sauce on the dinner
table. In 1917, cranberry grower Elizabeth Lee of New
Egypt, New Jersey, boiled some damaged cranberries
into jelly instead of throwing them away. The result?
The first cranberry sauce. She eventually teamed
up with two other cranberry growers to form what
would later become the Ocean Spray company,
making her tasty jelly available nationwide year-
round. Americans annually eat 80 million pounds of
cranberries during Thanksgiving week alone.

WELCOME TO YELLOW

If you know a little rudimentary Spanish,
you can figure out that "Los Angeles" translates to
"the angels," or "San Antonio" is "Saint Anthony."
Here are the meanings behind some other
US cities with Spanish names.

CITY: Modesto, California
MEANING: "Modest"

CITY: El Segundo, California
MEANING: "The Second"

CITY: Amarillo, Texas
MEANING: "Yellow"

CITY: El Cajon, California
MEANING: "The Box"

CITY: El Paso, Texas
MEANING: "The Pass" or "The Crossing"

CITY: Las Cruces, New Mexico
MEANING: "The Crosses"

AMERICA:
HOME OF THE
WORLD'S LARGEST . . .
CHEST OF DRAWERS

LOCATION: High Point, North Carolina

DETAILS: Honoring the region's reputation as the Furniture Capital of the World is this 80-foot-tall chest, built by the Furnitureland Store in 1926. Originally known as the Bureau of Information, today the chest also showcases two large neon socks hanging from an open drawer, representing High Point's hosiery industry.

Chance the Snapper

One tranquil evening in July 2019 at Humboldt Lagoon in West Chicago, onlookers saw something cutting a line across the water's still surface. There was no doubt about it: this was an alligator! Not a tiny one, either—it was at least five feet long. The sightings continued, and as photos of the gator made their way to social media and news sites, the questions mounted: How did it get there? (It was likely an illegal pet that grew too large.) Even more important: How could the city get it out of there? The reptile proved too smart for local wildlife officials, who failed to capture it after five days. By that point, it was a celebrity. Book Club Chicago held a naming contest; Ruth Gator Ginsberg and Frank Lloyd Bite lost out to Chance the Snapper, named for hometown music hero Chance the Rapper, who tweeted, "Just landed and found

out I gotta alligator." The Chicago Cubs sold Chance bobbleheads. The alligator's 15 minutes of fame even netted it a Wikipedia page.

But Chance wasn't leaving the 2.8-acre lagoon, and increasing crowd sizes forced him farther and farther into hiding. So Chicago enlisted the help of Frank Robb, who runs Crocodilian Specialist Services in St. Augustine, Florida. Showing the Midwesterners how it's done, the "gator whisperer" rowed out in the night and found Chance 25 yards from shore. Robb used a fishing rod with a large hook to snag the animal "like throwing a grapple hook over something." Then he reeled in the gator (the hook didn't harm it) and pulled it out by the tail. There was a bit of a struggle; at that point Robb had been awake for 36 hours, but as he said of Chance, "He was tired, too." Chicagoans were impressed, and Robb became just as famous as Chance: he also got a bobblehead. Robb even got to throw out the first pitch at a Cubs game. As for Chance, he retreated from the public eye and retired to Florida.

Dubya's Nicknames

Whether it was because of his sense of humor or because he had trouble remembering names, President George W. Bush used lots of nicknames for his associates. Here are a few of them.

BRITISH PRIME MINISTER TONY BLAIR: "Landslide." (Blair was elected prime minister in 1997 with a huge electoral victory.)

REP. FRED UPTON: "Freddo."

FEMA DIRECTOR JOE ALLBAUGH: "Big Country."

CIA DIRECTOR GEORGE TENET: "Brother George."

NATIONAL ENERGY POLICY DIRECTOR ANDREW D. LUNDQUIST: "Light Bulb."

MARY MATALIN, ASSISTANT TO THE VICE PRESIDENT: "M&M."

SPECIAL ASSISTANT TO THE PRESIDENT ISRAEL HERNANDEZ: One of his roles was providing the president with breath mints, so he earned the nickname "Altoid Boy."

DIRECTOR OF CIA COUNTERTERRORISM COFER BLACK: "Flies on the Eyeballs Guy."

BLOOMBERG NEWS REPORTER DICK KYLE: "Stretch." (He's tall.)

WASHINGTON TIMES REPORTER BILL SAMMON: "Super Stretch." (He's very tall—6'7".)

NBC NEWS REPORTER DAVID GREGORY: "Little Stretch." (He's not as tall—6'5".)

AMERICA'S STRANGEST RACES

Zombie Run

To qualify for this race, find an undead person and have them bite you. If there are no undead around, you can make yourself up to look like one. Or, if you prefer, you can dress up like a runner and try to outrun people dressed up like the undead. There are numerous zombie races in the US, and some of them go all out to put you in the experience. For example, the Zombie Run Escape in Perry, Georgia, looks like a location from *The Walking Dead*: participants must outrun brain-hungry zombies while navigating a ruined city—complete with collapsed buildings, a scary subway, an overturned school bus, and dozens of wrecked cars on a highway. As one runner raved, "It brought my favorite movies with zombie apocalypses to life!" Because who doesn't want that?

POLITICIANS SPEAK

A lot of presidential memoirs are,
they say, dull and self-serving.
I hope mine are interesting
and self-serving.

—Bill Clinton

STRANGE PLACES TO SPEND THE NIGHT

HUMAN NEST

LOCATION: Big Sur, California

DETAILS: Nestled among the cliffs and trees of this stunningly beautiful coastline, the environmentally friendly Treebones Resort boasts a "premier glamping experience." They offer the typical yurts and fancy tents and whatnot . . . and then there's the Human Nest. It sits in a craggy tree eight feet above the ground. Large enough to sleep two, the walls and roof are made of eucalyptus branches, hand-woven together by local artist Jayson Fann. Climb up the wooden ladder, settle into your futon, watch the sun disappear below the Pacific, and then sleep like a bird to the sounds of the surf.

BE SURE TO . . . set up a tent on the ground if rain is in the forecast, because the Human Nest isn't waterproof. And there's nothing in the Human Nest except a futon, so you have to climb the ladder with your pillows, sleeping bags, and any other belongings. Also, bring a lantern— it's basically a campsite in a tree. Cost: "$195. Two adult guests. Minimum two nights."

OVAL OFFICE FOODIES

★ George Washington's favorite dinner menu included cream of peanut soup, mashed sweet potatoes with coconut, string beans with mushrooms, and his wife's whiskey cake.

★ Abraham Lincoln's slender physique wouldn't lead anyone to believe he was a foodie, but his favorite dish was his wife's scalloped oysters.

★ Although each president has had a personal chef, Dwight Eisenhower preferred to cook his own beef stew.

★ Pity the poor Texan, Lyndon Johnson, who lived in our nation's capital with nary a Tex-Mex place (that he liked) in sight. He had to fly in caterers from Texas to get his hands on some proper Texas barbecue and chili.

★ Richard Nixon's culinary choices weren't exactly inspired—or inspiring! In keeping with the bland cooking of the late 1960s and early 1970s, Nixon often ate cottage cheese and ketchup, or

cottage cheese and pineapple, for lunch. His dinner of choice was Salisbury steak with gravy.

* Jimmy Carter liked Southern classics: a breakfast of grits and buttermilk, a dinner of country ham with redeye gravy or of fried chicken. The former peanut farmer also brought peanuts to a new level of worldwide notoriety.

* George H. W. Bush's dislike of broccoli was famous, but what isn't as well known is that Poppy had a sweet tooth. Stewards on *Air Force One* kept Eskimo Pies, Baby Ruth candy bars, and Blue Bell ice cream on hand for him.

* Bill Clinton's doctors worried that his increasing weight would adversely affect his health, but he never met a Big Mac he didn't like. (Though he did go vegan post-presidency.)

* Barack Obama ate lots of fresh veggies and healthy salmon, and kept a bowl of apples in the Oval Office for him and his guests to snack on. But he also enjoyed some cheat-day indulgences. One of his favorites was the Chili Half-Smoke from DC's famous Ben's Chili Bowl (which even features the president and First Lady on a mural painted outside the building).

WOODSTOCK EXPOSED

The Woodstock Music Festival—which ran from August 15–18, 1969, in Bethel, New York—remains one of the most iconic events of the 1960s hippie counterculture movement in America, and is remembered today as a

celebration of peace and love (albeit a muddy one without enough bathrooms). But the event actually began as a capitalist venture, a way for four local music promoters to make enough money to open a music studio. John Roberts, Joel Rosenman, Artie Kornfield, and Michael Lang managed to line up some of the most successful musical acts of the time—Jimi Hendrix, Jefferson Airplane, Janis Joplin, and others—and entice hundreds of thousands of young music lovers to pay between $18 and $24 each ($145 to $194 today) to see them perform. And don't think those artists played the show for free: the top performers were paid anywhere from $10,000 (Credence Clearwater Revival) to $18,000 (Jimi Hendrix) . . . and several of them—like Janis Joplin, the Grateful Dead, and the Who—refused to take the stage until they'd gotten their checks.

You Have Died of Dysentery

How much do you really know about the Oregon Trail?
For answers, turn to page 403.

1. **HOW MANY MODERN STATES CAN BE FOUND ALONG THE OREGON TRAIL?**
   a. Two
   b. Four
   c. Six
   d. Eight

2. **ON WHAT DATE DID THE FIRST OREGON TRAIL WAGON TRAIN SET OUT FOR THE WEST COAST?**
   a. June 3, 1840
   b. May 16, 1842
   c. March 13, 1850
   d. November 13, 1849

3. **WHAT PROMPTED MOST EARLY PIONEERS TO TRAVEL TO OREGON?**
   a. The weather was better than in the Midwest.
   b. They wanted free land.
   c. They wanted to move away from Native American settlements.
   d. They wanted to live close to the ocean.

4. **WHAT WAS THE MOST ESSENTIAL SUPPLY NEEDED ON THE TRAIL?**
   a. Food
   b. A gun
   c. A wagon
   d. All of the above

5. **WHAT WAS THE AVERAGE TRAVEL TIME FROM MISSOURI TO OREGON?**
   a. Two to three weeks
   b. Two to three months
   c. Four to six weeks
   d. Four to six months

6. WHAT WAS THE MOST DANGEROUS HAZARD THE PIONEERS FACED ON THEIR WAY TO OREGON?

   a. Attacks by Native Americans

   b. Cholera

   c. Sunstroke

   d. Runaway oxen

7. WHY DID TRAVELERS CIRCLE THEIR WAGONS?

   a. To protect themselves from attacks by Native Americans

   b. To keep children under control

   c. To corral livestock

   d. To protect themselves from bad weather

8. WHAT CAUSED TRAFFIC ON THE TRAIL TO DIMINISH?

   a. The Civil War

   b. Attacks by Native Americans

   c. The transcontinental railroad

   d. The invention of the telegraph

9. ABOUT HOW MANY PEOPLE TRAVELED OVER THE OREGON TRAIL?

   a. 350,000

   b. 500,000

   c. 875,000

   d. 1,000,000

10. WHEN DID THE OREGON TRAIL BECOME PART OF THE NATIONAL PARK SERVICE?

   a. 1900

   b. 1935

   c. 1954

   d. 1978

American Wit

Ninety-eight percent of the
adults in this country are decent,
hardworking, honest Americans.
It's the other lousy two percent
that get all the publicity.
But then, we elected them.

—LILY TOMLIN

WAITSTAFF RESTRICTIONS

Helen Herron Taft, wife of William Howard Taft, decreed that no bald-headed waiter or butler was permitted to serve in the White House. She felt that the previous occupants (Teddy Roosevelt and his wife, Edith) were too informal and lacking in dignity, and thought her new rule would create a favorable impression for guests. If this rule seems harsh, it was nothing compared to what came later: Lou Henry Hoover, wife of Herbert Hoover, insisted that all butlers, waiters, and footmen be exactly five feet, eight inches tall.

UNITED STATES OF SODA ... OR POP

⋆ The generic name for a soft drink varies by region: In New England and the Southwest, it's generally called "soda." In the Midwest and Pacific Northwest, it's generally "pop." And in Texas and the South, it's called "Coke" (even if it isn't Coca-Cola).

⋆ If you ever see a two-liter bottle of Coca-Cola at the store with a yellow cap, it's a special formula: it's kosher, brewed up for Passover.

⋆ Faygo is a popular soda (or pop) in the Midwest, produced in Michigan. It offers super-sweet flavors like Cotton Candy and Grape because the company's founders were previously bakers, and they based the flavors on frosting flavors.

⋆ In the 1960s, Dr Pepper was losing business in the winter. So it started a marketing campaign to teach consumers to drink Dr Pepper warm with a slice of lemon, like tea.

⋆ Soda with the most caffeine: Pepsi Zero Sugar, with 69 milligrams per 12-ounce serving. Legal FDA-imposed caffeine limit for soft drinks: 71 milligrams per 12-ounce serving. (Amount of caffeine in regular ol' Diet Pepsi: 36 milligrams.)

Half Dime

It's kind of odd that the nickel, or five-cent piece, is worth half as much as a dime, but is physically almost twice as large. It wasn't always that way. From 1792 to 1873, among the most widely used coins was the half dime. Made of silver, it was worth half a dime, or five cents. When five-cent pieces made of nickel alloy, or "nickels," came along in the 1860s, the half dime's time was up.

FIVE FREAKY FACTS ABOUT...
FICTIONAL AMERICANS

✶ Forrest Gump ran for 3 years, 2 months, 14 days, and 16 hours.

✶ Jason Bourne can speak English, French, Russian, Dutch, German, Swedish, Portuguese, and Spanish (and probably more).

✶ Batman's first big-screen appearance was in Andy Warhol's 1964 avant-garde film *Batman Dracula*. (No copies of the movie survive.)

✶ Buffy Summers, over the course of a feature film and two TV series, has slayed 133 vampires, 68 demons, 11 people, a spirit bear, and a robot.

✶ Before Freddy Krueger was killed and started invading teenagers' dreams, he was a serial killer known as the Springwood Slasher, who murdered at least 20 people.

More Tax Dollars at Work

★ In 2015, the Department of Defense spent $2 million on a new robot. One that will attack the enemy like the Terminator? Nope. This robot will just play a trumpet and improvise jazz music alongside human musicians.

★ Two grad students at the University of Washington received a $1.3 million grant from the National Science Foundation to study how foam beer-can holders known as "koozies" keep beer cold.

★ The National Science Foundation awarded $853,000 to Yakima Valley Community College in Washington state to expand its winemaking program. Community colleges cater largely to 18-to-20-year-olds, so some of the money will go toward serving alcohol . . . to minors.

★ The National Institute of Health spent $1 million testing the physiological response of the body to strenuous exercise. How? By putting 12 marmosets inside transparent hamster balls and making them run on a treadmill at increasing speeds. Three monkeys pooped in their balls; another vomited. (The National Institute on Aging spent $600,000 of taxpayer money on a similar study.)

A TEN-GALLON INVENTION

Most people consider the wide-brimmed hat worn by cowboys to be a quintessential symbol of the American west—and the name "Stetson" is synonymous with "cowboy hat." Before the Stetson, though, ranchers and cowboys wore whatever hats they happened to have, which could be anything from top hats to sailor caps.

During a hunting trip in the late 1850s, John B. Stetson made himself a hat (he knew what he was doing—his father was a hatmaker) with what he considered to be a comically large brim, but he soon realized that the brim was big enough to keep the sun (and rain) off his head and neck. In 1865, Stetson decided to start making the hats professionally. He rented a room in Houston, Texas; bought some tools and $10 worth of fur; and founded the Stetson Hat Company. Twenty years later, the company employed more than 1,100 people and manufactured hundreds of hats every day. Stetson died in 1906, but the company continued until it shut down in 1971, when it licensed the Stetson name to other hatmakers.

Continuing Adventures of Florida Man

BITE ME

Two Florida men were out for a stroll in Palm City one evening in October 2019 when they came across a small alligator. Noah Osborne, 22, captured the reptile with his bare hands. His friend, 27-year-old Timothy Kepke, decided that he wanted to get bitten by the alligator (no motive was given). The pair started filming the encounter on a cell phone, and Kepke grabbed the three-foot-long reptile and put its jaws around his forearm. But the gator didn't bite. It didn't do anything. Kepke shook it a bit, and then he poured his beer down the alligator's throat. The animal started thrashing about, and . . . the 19-second video ends. After Florida Fish and Wildlife officials saw the video online, Osborne and Kepke were charged with unlawfully taking an alligator, a felony. Kepke told police that he'd had only "a couple of beers" but wasn't drunk. He also said they released the animal unharmed (except for a mouthful of Coors).

Hidden in Plane Sight

During World War II, the Lockheed factory
in Burbank employed 80,000 people making
bombers for the war. But because it was so close
to the coast, the US government worried that
the factory was vulnerable to an enemy attack.
The solution? Camouflage the entire plant. One
problem: Lockheed was surrounded by tract
housing—not a forest or jungle, which might offer
easy camouflage. And so, this being Southern
California, the movie business came to the rescue.
Set designers and artists from studios including
Disney, Paramount, and 20th Century Fox covered
the factory and parking lot with a massive movie set
made largely of latex and chicken wire, disguised to
look like a typical Burbank neighborhood: houses,
streets, lawns, and cars. The factory's chimneys
and ventilation outlets became trees, bushes, and
fire hydrants. From the air, the whole setup was so
convincing that even a reconnaissance flight from
the US war department failed to identify the plant
among the surrounding suburbs.

Fly, Quetzalcoatlus ... Fly!

Today, Big Bend National Park in southwest Texas is a
rocky desert, but 67 million years ago, during the late
Cretaceous period, it was blanketed by forests. Soaring
above the trees was the largest flying creature that ever
lived: *Quetzalcoatlus*. Named after a Mesoamerican
feathered serpent god, one of these pterosaur's fossilized
wings was discovered in Big Bend in 1971. Proving things
really are bigger in Texas, this massive scavenger stood as
tall as a giraffe on land and was as wide as an F-16 fighter
jet in the air.

The biggest mystery about *Quetzalcoatlus* wasn't how
it could fly (its 34-foot wingspan could easily displace the
air to generate lift), but how it could take off. Without any
high cliffs to jump from, the pterosaur used "prehistoric
runways." Dr. Sankar Chatterjee, a paleontologist at
Texas Tech University, explains that "they'd have to run
but also need a downslope, a technique used today by
hang gliders." When their long, lumbering legs picked
enough speed, the leathery reptiles would flap harder
and harder until lift-off. "Once in the air, though, they
were magnificent gliders." To get a real sense of how
big these beasts really were, stand beneath the full-size
Quetzalcoatlus skeleton at the Big Bend Discovery Exhibit.

You Can't Eat Just One

This staple American snack food was born out of frustration. George Crum, the renowned head chef at Moon's Lake House in Saratoga Springs, New York, unwittingly made history in 1853 when a notoriously hard-to-please patron sent back a plate of french fries, complaining they were too thick. Fed up with the patron's complaints, Crum tossed several thin slices of potato into a pan, fried them to a crisp, and covered them with a generous helping of salt. To his surprise, the patron loved them, and Crum's "potato chips" soon became a staple on his menu. By the 20th century, potato chips had made their way into millions of American homes (and bellies).

SURFER SLANG

Whether you're riding the waves in Hawaii, California, or Florida, hang ten, moondoggie, and catch a wave of some surfer slang.

"AKAW!"
"Cool!"

ANKLE BUSTER
A wave that's too small to surf

BAGGIES
Surf shorts

BARNEY
An uncool or just plain bad surfer

BEACH LEECH
A surfer who doesn't have their own board and asks to borrow one from another surfer's quiver

BENNY
A non-local, or tourist surfer

BOMB
A gigantic wave

CLUCKED
When a surfer fears bombs

DAWN PATROL
Going surfing at sunrise

FRUBE
A surfer having such a bad time that he doesn't manage to catch a single wave all day

GLASS JOB
The fiberglass sheen on a surfboard

GOOFY FOOT
Most surfers ride with their left foot in front, and right in the back. Goofy foot is when they ride with the right in front.

GRAY BELLY
An old surfer

GROMMET
A kid surfer

GRUBBING
Wiping out (or falling off a surfboard)

HODAD
Somebody who hangs out on the beach all day but never surfs

HUMPBACK
When a big wave is followed by a smaller wave, and they form into one very big wave

JUICE
A wave's power

JUNKYARD DOG
A surfer with an awkward or unattractive surfing style

A MAN IN A GRAY SUIT
A shark. Also called Noah, and the Landlord.

MUSHBURGER
Flat, boring, impossible-to-surf waves that completely lack juice

PADDLEPUSS
A surfer too nervous to swim too far out, and who just paddles around near the shore

PARTY WAVE
A tasty wave big enough that it can be surfed by multiple people at the same time

QUIVER
A surfer's personal board collection

RAIL BANG
When a male surfer wipes out and the surfboard hits him hard . . . between the legs

REEF TAX
Cuts and bruises endured from surfing into rocks or a reef

THE SOUP
The ocean

SPONGER
A derisive term for a bodyboarder, or somebody who surfs by lying down on their board instead of standing up

A CITY OF SUPERLATIVES, PART III

The Big Apple isn't the only big-city nickname. For instance, there's...

ROCHESTER, THE FLOUR CITY: Flour milling was the biggest industry in this city in New York during the late 19th century.

MILWAUKEE, THE CREAM CITY: It has nothing to do with the dairy industry for which the rest of Wisconsin is famous. Red lacustrine clay is found in nearby lakes, and when it's fired, it turns from red to cream colored. Since the late 1800s, these cream colored bricks have been a popular building material in the Milwaukee area.

Washington's Smile

We've all heard the stories about George Washington's infamous wooden dentures. Poor George suffered from dental problems his entire adult life: he had his first tooth removed at age 24, and by the time of his presidential inauguration in 1789, when he was 57, he had just one tooth left. (That tooth was finally pulled in 1796 by Dr. John Greenwood, who was allowed to keep it as a memento—he wore it on his watch chain, encased in a small glass display.)

But "wooden" you know it? The claim that Washington's dentures were made of wood is just a myth. He used numerous full and partial dentures throughout his life, and they were constructed of various materials: human teeth (some were his own that he'd saved, and some were purchased), cow and horse teeth, ivory (possibly elephant), lead-tin alloy, silver alloy, and brass—but no wood. His last surviving set of dentures is still on display at Mount Vernon.

STRANGE TRIP

GIANT CORN MONUMENT

LOCATION: Dublin, Ohio

DETAILS: A field of giant concrete ears of corn, painted white, in a roadside plot in central Ohio. This work of art was created as a memorial to Sam Frantz, a local farmer who used the field from the 1930s until the 1960s to develop several strains of hybrid corn. It was commissioned by the City of Dublin Arts Council, and designed by Malcolm Cochran, an arts professor at Ohio State University. There are 109 concrete ears of corn in the field, which covers about two acres. Each of them is over six feet tall and weighs more than 1,500 pounds.

BONUS FACT: Locals have dubbed the site "Cornhenge."

Yellowstone's Big One

What is the largest volcano in the world?
Yellowstone National Park.

Beneath Yellowstone's meadows, hot pools, and mountain peaks lurks a molten monster. The entire park is a supervolcano, a volcano with the potential for massive eruptions. Yellowstone's caldera, or crater, is one of the largest in the world, encompassing 1,500 square miles. (By comparison, the Mt. St. Helens caldera is only two square miles.) The magma chamber that sits beneath the park and fuels its geysers, mud pots, and pools is three times the size of New York City. Bulges in the earth form and subside yearly, raising and lowering the elevation of the park's center. "The beast," as geologists call the volcano's magma, is stirring. Predicting volcanic activity is a tricky science, but researchers do say this: current geologic evidence suggests that Yellowstone erupts every 600,000 years; the last eruption was 630,000 years ago. Keep that in mind the next time you take a walk by Old Faithful.

POLITICIANS

SPEAK

Things are more

like they are now

than they ever were before.

—Dwight D. Eisenhower

Kentucky Fried Colonels

Harland Sanders—founder of the Kentucky Fried Chicken empire—isn't the only American to earn the honorary rank of "Kentucky colonel." In a tradition that dates back more than 200 years, Kentucky governors have commissioned more than 140,000 people "in recognition of noteworthy accomplishment and outstanding service to a community, state or nation." Two of the perks of being a Kentucky colonel: tickets to the Kentucky Derby and a special derby eve colonels' banquet, and the right to be addressed as "Honorable."

Other famous Kentucky colonels:

COLONEL TIGER WOODS	**COLONEL JOHNNY DEPP**
COLONEL SHIRLEY TEMPLE	**COLONEL HUNTER S. THOMPSON**
COLONEL BETTY WHITE	**COLONEL WHOOPI GOLDBERG**
COLONEL POPE JOHN PAUL II	**COLONEL WAYNE NEWTON**

One famous colonel who's not a Kentucky colonel is Colonel Tom Parker, Elvis Presley's longtime manager. Reason: He's a Louisiana colonel. In 1948, Parker was awarded a colonel's commission in the Louisiana State Militia by Governor Jimmie Davis, a former country singer who won his gubernatorial election with Parker's help in 1944. (Elvis, though, *was* a Kentucky colonel.)

The 14th Colony?

When the US established its constitution in 1787, the 13 former colonies became the new nation's first states. But there could have been 14, not 13. In 1785, a group of citizens in an isolated, sparsely populated mountainous region of western North Carolina called Franklin proposed creating their own state, predicated on the idea that doctors and lawyers were too highbrow—not representative of the common man—and thus unfit to serve in the legislature. Despite that weird premise for independence, 7 out of 13 states voted yes. Franklin was denied statehood by two votes. Nevertheless, Franklin's leading proponents acted like they had been granted statehood and proceeded to form a basic government: electing lawmakers (no doctors or lawyers allowed), establishing a court system, and assembling a small militia. All that local power wasn't enough to prevent attacks from nearby Native American tribes, who saw Franklin residents as easy targets. Because they'd behaved like a rogue state, North Carolina and the federal government left Franklin's residents to their own devices and offered no protection. In 1796, Franklin was absorbed into Tennessee.

BEASTLY PLACES

Love animals?
Consider moving to one of these US cities.

Turkey, Texas

Duck, West Virginia

Chicken, Alaska

Alligator, Mississippi

Sturgeon, Pennsylvania

Badger, Minnesota

Wild Horse, Colorado

Elk, Washington

Anaconda, Montana

Spider, Kentucky

Grey Eagle, Minnesota

Bumble Bee, Arizona

Pigeon, Michigan

Caribou, Maine

Hoot Owl, Oklahoma

Wildcat, Wyoming

Salmon, Idaho

Trout, Louisiana

Bison, South Dakota

Elephant, Pennsylvania

Antelope, California

Parrot, Georgia

Blue Heron, Kentucky

Flamingo, Florida

Tiger, Washington

Beaver, Alaska

Carp, Nevada

Dinosaur, Colorado

Rabbit Town, Maryland

Fox, Alaska

Pig, Kentucky

Partridge, Kansas

Coyote, New Mexico

Marlin, Texas

Lions, Louisiana

Pelican, Louisiana

Bear, Arizona

Crane, Missouri

Peacock, Michigan

Mustang, Oklahoma

Toad Suck, Arkansas

Wolverine, Michigan

Cougar, Washington

Mastodon, Michigan

Deer, Arkansas

Moose, Wyoming

Wolf, Wyoming

Otter, Montana

Carnivore Challenge

Feel like some pizza? Big Pie in the Sky Pizzeria in Kennesaw, Georgia, offers the Carnivore Challenge: in one hour, teams of two must eat every slice of a 30-inch, 11-pound pizza. Mandatory toppings include pepperoni, ground beef, Italian sausage, ham, and bacon.

The challenge costs $50 to attempt, but your team will split a $250 prize for finishing off the big pie. And judging by rule #2, the restaurant has had some problems with past challengers biting off more than they can chew:

> You cannot throw up, and if you do, you are responsible for any necessary cleanup! If you are going to throw up, do it outside, or make it to the bathroom. No one is going to clean up your personal mess nor should you expect them to, so use common sense. If you feel like you are going to throw up, stop eating and handle it! No one in the dining room wants to see that while they are eating . . .

Erik Unger and Anthony Reganato of Birmingham, Alabama, were first to complete the challenge, and six other teams followed—but none of them were able to beat Erik and Anthony's record time (33 minutes).

DOGS OF WAR

SERGEANT STUBBY

The most decorated dog of World War I is also the only canine to be promoted to sergeant through combat. Stubby, a stray, inadvertently volunteered for service in July 1917 by wandering onto the Yale University campus where the 102nd Infantry Regiment was training. After developing a fondness for the bull terrier mix, Corporal James Robert Conroy smuggled him aboard the troop ship when the unit was sent to France.

Stubby served for 18 months, participating in four offenses and 17 battles, suffering from two separate injuries and a mustard gas attack (after which he was outfitted with his own custom gas mask). In addition to aiding his fellow soldiers by warning them of gas attacks and incoming artillery

shells, and by locating missing soldiers (along with simply boosting morale), Stubby also single-handedly (err, single-*pawedly*) captured a German spy . . . by securely holding onto the enemy's posterior with his teeth.

Corporal Conroy smuggled Stubby back home at war's end, and Stubby quickly became a national celebrity. He was presented with a gold medal from the Humane Education Society by General John G. Pershing himself, and led parades, met Presidents Wilson, Coolidge, and Harding, and entertained crowds during halftime at Georgetown University's football games.

When Stubby died in his sleep in 1926, Conroy had a taxidermy of the dog created, which houses his cremains. Conroy donated Stubby to the Smithsonian Institute in 1956, and the dog is still on display today—in full uniform—at the National Museum of American History.

AMERICA:
HOME OF THE
WORLD'S LARGEST . . .
SHOE HOUSE

LOCATION: Hallam, Pennsylvania

DETAILS: In 1948, millionaire shoe manufacturer Mahlon N. Haines built this white house in the shape of a work shoe as an advertising gimmick for his company. It was a five-level working house—25 feet high, 48 feet long, with three bedrooms and two baths. Haines invited his employees to stay in it for their birthdays, anniversaries, and other special occasions; he also offered the house to any honeymooning couple from a town whose stores sold his shoes. (Nights in the shoe included full maid service, butler, cook, and chauffeur.)

Over the years, the Shoe House changed hands several times—it was an ice cream parlor for a while—but in 1987, Haines's granddaughter bought it and turned it into a museum dedicated to her grandfather.

Something's Fishy

CANDIDATE: Crawfish B. Crawfish, a boiled Louisiana crawfish

RUNNING FOR: President of the United States

CAMPAIGN NOTES: When Louisiana governor Bobby Jindal announced in June 2015 that he was running for president, someone who was definitely not one of Jindal's admirers created a Facebook group called "Can This Crawfish Get More Supporters Than Bobby Jindal?" and uploaded a photo of a boiled crawfish to the page. So many people clicked "like" on the photo that the creator decided to enter C. B. in the presidential race, where he continued to take shots at Jindal. (Jindal's campaign slogan: "Tanned. Rested. Ready." C. B. Crawfish's: "Red. Boiled. Ready.")

Jindal's popularity was at a low point when he launched his presidential campaign; being dogged by a dead, well-cooked, smart-alecky "Claw and Order candidate" didn't help. Jindal never rose above 1 percent in the polls and in one Fox News survey trailed dead last behind "None of the above." His campaign never caught on and in November 2015 he threw in the towel. One of the few bright spots in the race: he accumulated more than 250,000 followers on Facebook . . . and C. B. Crawfish topped out at 25,000.

REGIONAL TREAT

SLINGER

FOUND IN: St. Louis, Missouri

DESCRIPTION: A mountain of food similar to the Garbage Plate (see page 72). The Slinger consists of two eggs topped with hash browns and a hamburger patty. The whole thing is then covered in chili, topped with cheese and onions, and served with bacon or sausage.

The Memegwesi

The Chippewa Indians once inhabited Michigan, Wisconsin, Minnesota, North Dakota, and Ontario. Also referred to as Ojibwe, which means "Puckered Moccasin People," their landscape was dotted with tens of thousands of lakes and rivers—including the Great Lakes—so water played a huge part in their mythology.

According to Chippewa legend, the Memegwesi are a race of skinny, child-sized beings that live on riverbanks. Said to be made from the bark of trees, they are pale and hairy with six fingers on each hand; their large heads have glowing red eyes, and no nose. Their whiny voices might be mistaken for a dragonfly.

In some legends, the Memegwesi are mostly harmless, appearing only to a child or a shaman. But other tales paint them as vindictive little tricksters that hide below the rapids and capsize canoes. Leave them some tobacco and they might leave you alone. They're almost impossible for non-Indians to see, but if you look closely from the riverbank, you might spy the pictographs they left on the rocks.

Cape Canaveral...
er, Kennedy ... er, Canaveral

In 1961, President John F. Kennedy publicly gave
NASA a goal and the encouragement to meet that goal:
land a man (an *American* man) on the Moon by the end
of the decade. NASA did achieve the goal in 1969, but
Kennedy, who was assassinated in November 1963,
didn't live to see it happen. Shortly after Kennedy's
death, his widow, Jacqueline Kennedy, suggested to
the new president, Lyndon B. Johnson, that a good
way to memorialize JFK would be to rename NASA's
Launch Operations Center in Cape Canaveral, Florida,
in his honor. Johnson went one better, renaming the
entire area after the president. Less than a week after
the assassination, on Thanksgiving 1963, Johnson
announced that Cape Canaveral would be renamed
Cape Kennedy. The Department of the Interior (which
has to approve name changes) supported the change,
but locals never much liked having the region renamed
without their input. Ten years later, the Florida state
legislature passed a law that renamed Cape Kennedy . . .
Cape Canaveral.

American
Wit

Americans will

put up with anything

provided it doesn't block traffic.

—DAN RATHER

THE CITY OF SOULS

*Colma would be one of
California's most populous cities...
if its residents were alive.*

FAMOUS "RESIDENTS": Colma hosts 17 cemeteries
and crematoriums. Baseball great Joe DiMaggio
and one of San Francisco's most famous murder
victims, Mayor George Moscone (assassinated in
1978 along with activist Harvey Milk), are buried at
Holy Cross Catholic Cemetery. Wyatt Earp rests in the
Hills of Eternity. William Randolph Hearst's grave
is at Cypress Lawn Memorial Park. Also at Cypress
Lawn: Harry "the Horse" Flamburis, a former Hells
Angels gang leader whose pals supposedly buried his
chopper with him.

CLAIM TO FAME: Located just south of San Francisco
in San Mateo County, Colma is known as the "City of
Souls" because it has fewer than 2,000 live residents,
but nearly 2 million "at rest." Colma's Japanese,
Chinese, Italian, Serbian, Catholic, Jewish, Greek
Orthodox, and nondenominational cemeteries all

have their origins in the pricy city to the north. In the late 1880s, San Francisco's cemeteries were nearly full, but real estate was becoming more and more expensive. So city residents turned to nearby Colma, an easy carriage ride to the south. The first cemetery opened in 1887, and in 1914 (because many old cemeteries were deteriorating), many of San Francisco's dead were moved to mass graves in Colma, which became the city's necropolis.

MORE STRANGE LAWS

* In Christiansburg, Virginia, it's a crime to imitate the sound of a police whistle.

* It's against the law in Iowa to charge people to watch a one-armed pianist perform.

* In Missouri, men are legally required to have a permit to shave.

* It's a crime in Long Beach, California, to curse while playing miniature golf.

* A man may not legally wear a strapless evening gown in Miami.

FIRST IN TOMATO PIES

Americans love their pizza pies! New York grocery store owner Gennaro Lombardi received the first American merchant license for a pizzeria in 1905. Back then, pizza was called tomato pie, and ingredients were piled upside down, with the cheese on the bottom, then anchovies (the only topping available), and the sauce last. A whole pie was five cents, but Lombardi's would sell smaller pieces based on how much customers wanted to spend. The pie (or piece) was then wrapped in paper and tied with string.

American Giant

In 1925, the Minnesota Valley Canning Company—
specialists in canned vegetables—introduced what
became its signature product: an unusually large, sweet,
and tender pea called "Green Giant." The company
hired the Leo Burnett advertising agency to come up
with a campaign to promote the product, and the Green
Giant, a symbol to represent the new pea, was born. The
original giant was not the pleasant icon we now know:
he was "stooped, scowling, wore a scruffy bearskin and
looked more like the Incredible Hulk than the happy
gardener he is today."

There was just one problem: this angry giant was
scaring the very children who were supposed to eat
his products. So, in the mid-1930s, he underwent a
makeover: his scowl was replaced with a smile, his
posture improved, and he donned new leafy clothes. The
company added the word "jolly" to his name and gave
him his signature "Ho ho ho" utterance. The Jolly Green
Giant ended up bringing his company so much success
that, in 1950, the Minnesota Valley Canning Company
rebranded as "Green Giant" and trademarked the name
to represent all its products. The iconic spokesman has
since become a "giant" in the advertising world.

Magichigans

After purchasing a summer home in Colon with his wife in 1926, famed illusionist Harry Blackstone made many appearances (and disappearances) around Michigan, wowing audiences with his tricks. A long-running battle of wits with rival magician Howard Thurston unfolded during the 1920s. Gradually, Blackstone gained the upper hand,

although it is rumored that he may have "spirited away" many of his competitor's original tricks: when Thurston accused him of imitating his assistant-sawing trick, Blackstone responded, "It's true. I did catch your act in Philadelphia. But you did it so poorly, I wouldn't try to imitate you."

In 1927, Blackstone invited Australian conjuror Percy Abbott to his home for a vacation, which resulted in Abbott's relocation to the area. The magicians opened Colon's first magic business, the Blackstone Magic Company, in 1927. After the partnership dissolved, Abbott opened a new store, Abbott's Magic Manufacturing Company, in 1934. The open house he held in 1935 brought dozens of magicians together to socialize, buy supplies, and watch magic acts. The Abbott's Get Together, now a renowned magicians' convention, is still held every August, and Abbott's Magic has become the world's largest manufacturer of magic supplies. Thanks to Blackstone and Abbott, Colon is now known as the "Magic Capital of the World."

ABE LINCOLN, FASHION ICON?

When Abraham Lincoln was still a presidential hopeful, he opened his mail one day—October 18, 1860, to be exact—and found this piece of advice from 11-year-old Grace Bedell of Westfield, New York. Give up shaving, she told him, and you've got it in the bag. Wrote Grace:

> You would look a great deal better for your face is so thin . . . All the ladies like whiskers and they would tease their husbands to vote for you and you would be President.

Abe dashed off this reply:

> As to the whiskers, having never worn any, do you not think people would call it a piece of silly affectation if I were to begin now?

Despite his answer to Grace, the little girl's suggestion must have played on his mind. Lincoln loved to have his picture taken and—fortunately for history—we can unmistakably chronicle the progression of his beard:

* November 26, 1860—a thin scraggly line of whiskers appears

* January 26, 1861—more growth, but still scraggly

* February 9, 1861—a mature, full growth of facial hair adorns the face of—ta-da!— President Abraham Lincoln

Thanks to Grace Bedell, Abraham Lincoln became the first US president to sport facial hair of any kind. He must have started a trend: ten of the next 11 presidents wore beards or sidewhiskers, with or without mustaches.

STANDARD TIME

You may think standard time—the synchronizing of all clocks within one region—was a government creation, but it was actually invented by a railroad man. William Allen of South Orange, New Jersey, had been working on railroads since the age of 16. He devised this timekeeping system to help synchronize train schedules across the United States. It was adopted at the 1875 General Time Convention, but the US Congress didn't make standard time official until 1919.

FIVE FREAKY FACTS ABOUT ...
MINNESOTA

★ Coniferous forest covers 40 percent of the state.

★ Per International Falls law, cats may not chase dogs up telephone poles.

★ The first skyway (an enclosed pedestrian bridge connecting buildings above street level) went up in Minneapolis in 1962. Today, the city has more than nine miles of skyways connecting 80 city blocks—the largest such system in the world.

★ Burnsville is home to the Eagle Magic and Joke Store, America's oldest magic shop. That's no trick—they've been open since 1900.

★ Minnesota is one of only four states with an official muffin. (It's blueberry.)

31 FLAVORS

Brothers-in-law Burt Baskin and Irv Robbins
open the first Baskin-Robbins ice cream parlor
in Glendale, California, in 1945,
famously offering ice-cream
lovers a choice of "31 flavors."
It's grown to more than
2,400 nationwide (and more
than 6,700 international)
locations thanks to its huge
menu of creative choices—
more than 1,400 total
flavors so far. So why did
they start with 31 flavors? First,
that's one flavor for every day of
the month. Second, it was a way to
one-up (or three-up) the chain that
was their big rival in 1945: Howard
Johnson's, which offered 28.

POLITICIANS **SPEAK**

I know I am getting better at golf because I am hitting fewer spectators.

—GERALD FORD

STOP
in the Name
of the Law

For years, residents of the Chicago suburb of Oak Lawn complained that motorists don't come to a complete stop at stop signs. So in 2007, Mayor Dave Heilmann came up with a creative solution: he added a second, smaller octagonal sign below 50 of the town's stop signs with a witty line. So, for example, drivers would see:

STOP
AND SMELL THE ROSES

Other signs read "STOP right there, pilgrim," "STOP billion dollar fine," and "STOP in the naaaame of love." The Illinois Department of Transportation deemed the signs violations of the Federal Uniform Traffic Control Act and threatened to withhold funds for road projects if the signs weren't removed. Heilmann complied, but complained, "I think government needs to take itself less seriously."

PARANORMAL PARKS, PART III

America's national parks are full of ghostly tales...

OLD GREEN EYES: CHICKAMAUGA AND CHATTANOOGA NATIONAL MILITARY PARK, GEORGIA AND TENNESSEE

From Gettysburg to Antietam to the Great Smoky Mountains, Civil War ghosts abound. But none is so eerie as "Old Green Eyes," the bodiless Confederate spirit who haunts Chickamauga Creek in Georgia. Chickamauga and the nearby town of Chattanooga, Tennessee, were strategic Union strongholds during the Civil War. If Confederate soldiers had captured the area, they easily could have pushed into Union territory.

In September 1863, the Confederates did take Chickamauga, but two months later, a Union victory at Chattanooga prevented the rebels from moving into Tennessee. More than 40,000 soldiers died in the battles; one of those was Old Green Eyes (no one knows what his real name was). The soldier was decapitated during the battle at Chickamauga: only his head was found. It was buried on the battlefield and, according to residents, continues to haunt the area. Locals and visitors claim to have seen the spirit head—recognizable by its glowing green eyes—moaning and wandering the battlefield searching for its missing body.

The Jellybean President

During Ronald Reagan's years at the White House,
a jar of jellybeans could always be found in the Oval
Office, on *Air Force One*, and in the Cabinet meeting
rooms. The president began his love affair with the
chewy candy when he stopped smoking in the late
1960s. Jellybeans helped ease his nicotine cravings;
licorice was his favorite flavor. At about the same time,
the Rowland family, California candy makers and
devout Republicans, began sending the then-governor
of California a 20-pound shipment of jellybeans every
month to help him kick the tobacco habit.

In 1976, the Rowlands went on to introduce the Jelly
Belly brand to the world. Jelly Belly jellybeans looked
like ordinary jellybeans, but their gourmet flavors
were out of this world. To honor him when he became
president, Jelly Belly sent Reagan 7,000 pounds of red,
white, and blue jellybeans for his 1981 inauguration.
The blueberry jellybean was invented just for the
occasion. (They needed a bean in just the right shade of
blue.) Reagan loved the patriotic beans, but licorice still
remained his favorite.

SHORTEST PLACE NAMES IN THE UNITED STATES

Kentucky, what gives?

Y, Alaska

AI, Ohio

ED, Kentucky

OZ, Kentucky

TB, Maryland

TI, Oklahoma

UZ, Kentucky

THE FAMILY CIRCUS

It's one of America's most iconic comic strips. There's the old adage that smart writers who want to get things done "write what they know," and cartoonist Bil Keane did just that with *The Family Circus*. In 1960, he started drawing a daily, single-panel sweet and sentimental strip based on his home life with his wife Thelma and their five children. He turned his five kids into four characters, combining sons Billy and Chris into "Billy," son Jeff into "Jeffy," baby P. J. into "P. J.," and daughter Gayle into "Dolly," which was Thelma Keane's nickname for all little girls. Like the real Keanes, the comic family lives in Scottsdale, Arizona, with a stay-at-home mom and a dad who works as a cartoonist. The strip still runs today—the real Jeff Keane took over after Bil Keane's death in 2011—but there have been some changes. For its first few years, the dad was named Steve, not Bil, and the strip was titled *The Family Circle* because it was encased in a black circle. (It had to be changed after *Family Circle* magazine threatened to sue.)

Poor Richard

Between 1732 and 1758, Benjamin Franklin published an annual almanac—he took the pseudonym "Poor Richard" and called the publication **Poor Richard's Almanack.** *These famous phrases attributed to Franklin came from that work.*

"Fish and visitors stink after three days."

"God helps them that help themselves."

"The noblest question in the world is: What good can I do in it?"

"A good example is the best sermon."

"They who can give up essential liberty to obtain a little temporary safety deserve neither liberty nor safety."

"There was never a good war or a bad peace."

"He that lieth down with dogs shall rise up with fleas."

"Work as if you were to live a hundred years, pray as if you were to die tomorrow."

"To err is human, to forgive divine; to persist devilish."

"Nothing can be said to be certain, except death and taxes."

"He that is good for making excuses is seldom good for anything else."

"People who are wrapped up in themselves make small packages."

"So convenient a thing it is to be a reasonable creature, since it enables one to find or make a reason for everything one has a mind to do."

"Old boys have their playthings as well as young ones; the difference is only in the price."

"He that teaches himself, hath a fool for his master."

"Three may keep a secret, if two of them are dead."

"Early to bed and early to rise makes a man healthy, wealthy, and wise."

AMERICA:
HOME OF THE
WORLD'S LARGEST . . .
THERMOMETER

LOCATION: Baker, California

DETAILS: At the "gateway to Death Valley," one of the hottest places on Earth, stands this working thermometer. The original steel electric sign was commissioned in 1991, but was rebuilt in 1993 after 70-mile-per-hour winds snapped it in half. Electric bills of $8,000 per month forced the owner at the time to turn off the thermometer in 2012, but an official relighting (under new ownership) took place in 2014. The structure is 134 feet high and is capable of registering temperatures up to 134 degrees Fahrenheit—commemorating the highest temperature ever recorded in Death Valley (in 1913).

One Dangerous Balloon

When the Macy's department store launched its beloved annual Thanksgiving Day Parade in 1924, the procession included marching bands, floats, Santa Claus, and a collection of animals from the Central Park Zoo. The giant balloons that have come to be a signature of the celebration were introduced in 1927 to replace the zoo animals (they were scaring too many children). At the end of the parade, the balloons were released into the air.

The next year, Macy's started placing a return address label to each balloon and offering a $100 reward to anybody who returned one. In 1931, Colonel Clarence E. Chamberlain managed to capture a stray balloon on his airplane's wing. Despite a ban on airplane retrieval that went into effect after that, in 1932, another pilot attempted the same feat—and nearly crashed his plane. That was the last year Macy's released their balloons.

BONUS FACT: The parade was canceled from 1942 to 1944 because of a wartime shortage of both rubber and helium.

STATE OF THE UNION

The Labor Relations Act of 1935 allows American laborers to form unions and maintain union membership without retaliation from employers. Today, the Teamsters (officially called the International Brotherhood of Teamsters) is one of the largest unions in the United States and represents 1.2 million workers nationwide, including truck drivers, chauffeurs, warehouse workers, and more. But the name reflects the group's early years as a union that represented a specific group of workers: delivery drivers who commanded teams of oxen or mules.

FIVE FAVORITE AMERICAN CHEFS AND THE FOODS THEY HATE

1. **GUY FIERI:** eggs

2. **INA GARTEN:** cilantro

3. **RACHAEL RAY:** store-bought mayonnaise

4. **REE DRUMMOND:** bananas

5. **GIADA DE LAURENTIIS:** coconut

A BOUNCE FOR PILOTS

When World War II started, George Nissen, the inventor of the trampoline, convinced the Army that trampolines could train pilots to not only achieve better balance but also to be less fearful of being upside down. And jumping on a trampoline was great for physical conditioning. The military agreed; thousands of cadets learned to jump on trampolines.

Poor Baby

*According to the Social Security Administration,
these are some of the least popular baby names
in the United States through the years.*

BOYS	GIRLS
Arvid (1880)	Ula (1880)
Pomp (1893)	Medie (1893)
Bubber (1900)	Algie (1900)
Bunion (1917)	Etola (1917)
Ramona (1930)	Lanta (1930)
Dink (1944)	Mliss (1944)
Esco (1957)	Romanita (1957)
Heidi (1965)	Elfida (1965)
Roozbeh (1978)	Earlean (1978)
Travious (1986)	Ita (1986)
In (1992)	Floyd (1992)
Dinero (2005)	Copper (2005)
Henos (2018)	Diti (2018)

WAKANDA EXPORTS

In 2019, a software engineer named Francis Tseng was researching agricultural tariffs on the US Department of Agriculture's website. While looking through a list of the nation's trade partners, he came across a country that left him, as he later told Reuters, "very confused." It was Wakanda, the fictional sub-Saharan African country where Marvel superhero Black Panther lives. At first, Tseng thought he "misremembered" the name. Yet there it was—Wakanda—complete with a list of exports to the United States, including "ducks, donkeys, and dairy cows." A USDA official later explained that Black Panther's homeland was "added to the list by accident during a staff test" and has since been removed.

When Barry Met Michelle

More stories of how our presidents and First Ladies met.

WHEN RONNIE MET NANCY

Ronald Reagan wrote in his autobiography that he first met Nancy Davis when she came to him for help. He was president of the Screen Actors Guild, and she couldn't get a job acting in movies because another Nancy Davis's name had shown up on the Hollywood blacklist of alleged communists. But according to Jon Weiner's book *Professors, Politics, and Pop*, SAG records show that Nancy's blacklist problem occurred in 1953—a year after the Reagans were married. So how did they meet? Reagan biographer Anne Edwards says that in 1949, Nancy, who had just become an MGM contract player, told a friend of Reagan's that she wanted to meet him. The friend invited both to a small dinner party, and the rest is history.

WHEN BARRY MET MICHELLE

In 1989, Michelle Robinson was working at a Chicago law firm when she was assigned to mentor a summer associate from Harvard with a "strange name"—Barack Obama. Not long after, Barack, 27, asked Michelle, 25, on a date. She later admitted that she was reluctant to date one of the few Black men at the large firm because it seemed "tacky." Robinson finally relented, and after dating for several months, she suggested they get married. He wasn't interested. One night in 1991, during dinner at a Chicago restaurant, she brought it up again. Again, he said no. But when dessert showed up, there was an engagement ring in a box on one of the plates. They were married in 1992.

STRANGE PLACES TO SPEND THE NIGHT

A Metal Box at a Hot Spring

LOCATION: The Alvord Desert in southeastern Oregon

DETAILS: One of the most remote spots in the West, the Alvord Desert is tucked into the base of Steens Mountain (elev. 9,734 feet). This creates a rain shadow that keeps the 11-mile-long playa completely flat—so flat that land-speed world records have been set there.

The geothermally active area has dozens of hot springs. The only one safe enough to soak in (thanks to temperature regulators) is privately owned at a rustic campground that includes a half dozen "MASH" units. Short for Mobile Alvord Sleeping Huts, these long metal boxes were once shipping containers that rode on flatbed trucks. Each non-insulated unit comes with a bed, a table, a light, and not much else. Getting in and out requires lifting a big metal lever that opens the wall-sized door. They're just a short walk from the developed hot spring where guests can soak the night away under the brightest Milky Way you've ever seen.

BE SURE TO . . . see the playa. Campers get access to a private road to the Alvord Desert, which is really, really fun to drive on (just watch out for those land-speed record attempters).

WHAT A VIEW!

These states have the most ocean coastline.

1. **ALASKA:** 6,640 miles

2. **FLORIDA:** 1,350 miles

3. **CALIFORNIA:** 840 miles

4. **HAWAII:** 750 miles

5. **LOUISIANA:** 397 miles

6. **TEXAS:** 367 miles

7. **NORTH CAROLINA:** 301 miles

8. **OREGON:** 296 miles

PROJECT BLUE BOOK

Between 1947 and 1969, the US military sponsored Project Blue Book—a secret operation to investigate UFO activity in the United States. Over the course of 22 years, project officials looked into 12,618 reports of UFO sightings. Most of those were discounted as hoaxes or natural events (like stars or lightning). But 701 reports remain unexplained.

NATIONAL DEBT CLOCK

In the winter of 1980, New York real estate developer Seymour Durst wanted to communicate his concerns about the ballooning national debt to elected officials in Washington, DC. So he sent them New Year's cards that read "Happy New Year! Your share of the national debt is $35,000." No response—so Durst went to a sign maker and asked if it was possible to make a billboard with a numeric display that showed the national debt growing in real time—a doomsday clock for the American taxpayer. It wasn't possible: That year, the debt was growing at a rate of about $13,000 per second, and the computers of the day weren't fast enough to operate a numeric display at that kind of speed. It took eight years for technology to catch up with Durst's vision, and in 1989, the first National Debt Clock was installed on a Durst-owned building near Times Square. Cost: $100,000. (No word on whether Durst went into debt to pay for the clock.)

Each week Durst called the US Treasury to get the latest national debt figures and updated the sign via modem so that the continuously changing numbers were as accurate as possible. He continued updating the clock until his death in 1995, after which the sign company assumed the responsibility. In 2000, the national debt stopped growing, and for the next two years it actually shrank. That created a problem for the sign, which wasn't designed to run backward. On Durst's birthday in 2000, the sign was switched off and covered with a red, white, and blue banner in the hope that it would never be uncovered.

But the debt soon started rising again, and in July 2002 the sign was switched back on. It was replaced with a new, improved sign in 2004, but the new sign wasn't "improved" enough: When the national debt hit $10 trillion in 2008, there weren't enough digits to display all the debt, and the "$" had to be converted to a 1. (That 1 is up to a 3 at the time of this writing.)

Headlines, Florida Style

Florida Man Arrested for Calling 9-1-1 after His Cat Was Denied Entry into Strip Club

ANOTHER PERSON SEEN CLINGING TO CAR HOOD ON I 95 IN MIAMI

FLORIDA MAN ON DRUGS KILLS IMAGINARY FRIEND AND TURNS HIMSELF IN

Hardware Store Discards 15 Feet of Carpet after Florida Man Rolls Himself Up in It and Pees

8-hour Standoff Ends after Palm Harbor Man Tells Police He Was Shooting at Rats in His Backyard

Florida Man Charged with Assault with a Deadly Weapon after Throwing Alligator through Wendy's Drive-Thru Window

Florida Man Calls 9-1-1 During Police Chase, Asks for Donald Trump

Thousands of Gun Owners in Florida Planning to "Shoot Down" Hurricane Irma

FLORIDA MAN WRECKS LIQUOR SHOP, BLAMES "HOOKAH-SMOKING CATERPILLAR" FROM *ALICE IN WONDERLAND*

Florida Man Stuffing Fish down Pants in Pet Store Theft Caught on Camera

TAMPA TEACHER ARRESTED FOR DRUNKENLY LETTING A 14-YEAR-OLD BOY DRIVE HER TO WAFFLE HOUSE

Cape Coral "Off-the-Grid" Woman Thought George Michael's Song "Faith" Would Heal Dog

NO LAUGHING MATTER

Snoopy, Charlie Brown, and the rest of the *Peanuts* gang have been making Americans laugh since the comic debuted in 1950. But the beloved Charlie Brown TV specials include no actual laughs. Charles Schulz, the comic's creator, insisted that viewers should be able to enjoy the cartoons and not be told when to laugh. CBS network executives did create a version of *A Charlie Brown Christmas* with a laugh track in case Schulz ever came around to their way of thinking. But he didn't, and the laugh-track version was never aired.

One Large Pizza with Extra Cicadas

*Think people only eat bugs in other parts of the world,
not in the Strange USA? Think again!*

★ Of the trillions of Brood X cicadas that emerged
after a 17-year slumber and swarmed the Midwest in
2020, a few ended up on pizza: the fancy-schmancy
"Spicy Thai Cicada Pie" crafted at Pizza Bandit in
Dayton, Ohio. Featuring "blanched and sautéed
locally foraged cicadas" (that Pizza Bandit wasn't sure
they could legally serve), this one-time-only offering
(with cicada wings on the crust) got mixed reviews.
Per Facebook, "Opinions of the pizza range from
absolutely delicious to . . . well . . . uh . . . yeah . . ."

★ The Canyon Hopper pizza "started out as a joke
amongst our stoner friends," reads a post from Evel
Pie in Las Vegas. Above-average spring rainfall caused
a biblical swarm of grasshoppers to invade Sin City in
2019. Taking the stoners' advice, the pizzeria (which
honors Evel Knievel, America's famous daredevil)
roasted the grasshoppers with lime and garlic, then
added them to a pie topped with chorizo, goat cheese,
caramelized onions, and arugula. Calling the pizza
"damn good," they did warn that it's "only for the
bravest of daredevils."

Defining the States

These states took their names from the
Native American languages spoken in their regions.

ALABAMA: "clears the thicket" (Choctaw)

ALASKA: "mainland" (Aleut)

ARIZONA: "small springs" (O'odham)

DAKOTA: "friendly" (Siouan)

CONNECTICUT: "at the long tidal river" (Algonquin)

ILLINOIS: "many men" (Algonquin)

KANSAS: "people of the south wind" (Siouan)

KENTUCKY: "on the meadow" (Iroquoian)

MASSACHUSETTS: "at the great hill" (Algonquin)

MICHIGAN: "large lake" (Algonquin)

MINNESOTA: "white water" (Siouan)

MISSISSIPPI: "big river" (Algonquin)

MISSOURI: "people of the large canoes" (Algonquin)

NEBRASKA: "flat water" (Siouan)

OHIO: "good river" (Iroquoian)

OKLAHOMA: "red people" (Choctaw)

TEXAS: "allies" (Caddo)

UTAH: "high" (Athabaskan)

WISCONSIN: "it lies red" (Algonquin)

WYOMING: "at the big river flat" (Algonquin)

FAST-FOOD FOUNDERS
Jack in the Box

NOW: Jack in the Box is one of the nation's largest hamburger chains, with more than 2,200 restaurants in 21 states.

THEN: In 1941, Robert Oscar Peterson founded Topsy's drive-in restaurant in San Diego. Over the next decade, he opened several more Topsy's, which he renamed Oscar's, creating a chain of drive-ins in Southern California with whimsical circus-like decor. Then in 1951, Peterson remodeled the original Topsy's into a Jack in the Box. The major change was an intercom placed inside "Jack" the clown, allowing drivers to talk directly to the service crew to place an order. Many customers weren't used to drive-throughs back then, though, so signs directed them to "pull up to Jack and place your order." Peterson eventually converted all of his restaurants to drive-throughs, and the fact that patrons just picked up their food and drove off helped Peterson keep his overhead costs low. It also helped revolutionize fast food as other chains took up the idea.

PRICE OF POSTAGE

As part of the 2008 economic stimulus package, the IRS decided to inform citizens that their checks were coming, so they sent out letters to 130 million taxpayers. Cost of sending the letters: $42 million. A few weeks later the IRS spent that amount again to send the real checks.

STEAK YOURSELF TO A FREE MEAL

Even the appetites are bigger in Texas. Billboards leading to the Big Texan Steak Ranch in Amarillo, Texas, offer a "Free 72-oz steak!" For a $50 fee, anyone can try their hand at polishing off an entire 72-ounce steak dinner—if they're successful, the meal is free. Contestants have just 60 minutes to eat the steak (which is a whopping four and a half pounds of meat), along with a shrimp cocktail, salad, baked potato, and

dinner roll. Want to try? There are a few rules: once you start eating, you may not leave the table for any reason; you must cut your own meat (nobody else can assist you with the meal); if you upchuck, the contest is over; and if you don't finish the meal, you're not allowed to share it.

Of the more than 28,600 hearty eaters who've attempted the challenge since it began in 1960, more than 4,780 have succeeded. The overall odds of failing are 6 to 1 (but of the four or five women who try annually, about half succeed—so the success rate is a bit higher for the ladies). Winners get their names in the Steak Eater's Hall of Fame. Some standouts include professional wrestler Klondike Bill (who finished two 72-ouncers in the allotted time), a pitcher for the Cincinnati Reds rumored to have downed the entire meal in just over 9 minutes, a 69-year-old grandmother (the oldest person to finish), and an 11-year-old boy (the youngest).

AMERICA:
HOME OF THE
WORLD'S LARGEST . . .
TERMITE

LOCATION: Providence, Rhode Island

DETAILS: This 58-foot-long insect sits on the roof of a pest control company's building on the southbound side of I-95. "Nibbles Woodaway" (named in a local radio contest) was built in 1980 at a cost of $30,000, and is 928 times the size of an actual termite—which makes it clearly visible from the interstate. The company that created Nibbles was formerly called New England Pest Control, but changed its name to Big Blue Bug Solutions in 2012 in honor of its longtime mascot.

BONUS FACT: Nibbles is hurricane-proof, and made out of fiberglass, so it's termite-proof.

WHY'D THEY CALL IT THAT?

Yellowstone National Park, Wyoming/Montana/Idaho

Yellowstone National Park warns visitors with Death Gulch, so named because toxic gas from vents in the gulch once caused the death of six bears, one elk, and lots of smaller critters and insects. The Stygian Caves, named for the River Styx of Greek mythology, killed any bird or animal that got too close to the poisonous gases that rise from their openings. Electric Peak is a reminder of the danger of lightning strikes: in 1872, surveyor Henry Gannett was ascending the peak when an electric storm came up, causing his hair to stand on end.

THE UNINTELLIGENCE AGENCY

Two years after the September 11, 2001, terror attacks, Dennis Montgomery, a 57-year-old software developer, offered the CIA a way to catch al-Qaeda. He told them he'd developed software at his Nevada company that could unscramble terrorist messages hidden among the pixels on Al Jazeera's news channel. The CIA awarded Montgomery $20 million in government contracts without even testing the software. It turned out to be completely bogus—Montgomery was simply a tech geek trying to con the government. He wasn't prosecuted, and all information regarding the incident has been classified to avoid any further embarrassment to the CIA.

FIVE FREAKY FACTS ABOUT...
NEW JERSEY

★ There are 1,500 types of insect that make their homes in the average backyard in northern New Jersey.

★ Residents consume more than 1 million ice cream cones each summer.

★ New Jersey has more nail salons per capita than any other state, and more horses per square mile.

★ Gloucester County is home to the nation's oldest log cabin (Nothnagle Log House, built between 1638 and 1643), and the nation's oldest brick house (known as both Candor Hall and Ladd's Castle, built in 1688).

★ It's illegal for ducks to quack after 10:00 pm in Essex Fells. (Though there's no word on who pays the fine when an animal runs "a-fowl" of this law.)

PIZZA SAVES LIVES

Kirk Alexander ordered pizza from a Salem, Oregon, Domino's several times a week for more than a decade. In May 2016, however, he hadn't placed an order in 11 days . . . and the employees at Domino's started to worry that something might be wrong with him. So they sent a delivery driver to Alexander's home. When the driver got there, she could see that the lights and TV were on, but no one answered the door. She called Alexander's number and, after getting his voice mail, decided to call 9-1-1. Good move. Marion County sheriff's deputies arrived, entered the home, and found a weakened Alexander calling for help. He had suffered a medical emergency (no word on whether it was pizza-related) and was taken by paramedics to a hospital. According to a police spokesman, if Domino's hadn't checked in on him, he could have died.

Dueling Dems

In 1859, Senator David Broderick of California, a power broker in the Democratic Party's antislavery faction, was challenged to a duel by political enemy and proslavery activist David Terry, California's chief justice. They met at dawn at Lake Merced, south of San Francisco. Broderick had the first shot, but when his gun misfired, Terry calmly put a bullet through Broderick's chest. Broderick now has the unique distinction of being the only US senator to be killed in a duel while in office. Terry was tried for murder and acquitted, and three years later he joined the Confederate army. In 1889, the elderly Terry was gunned down by the bodyguard of Supreme Court justice Stephen Field after Terry confronted Field in a train station restaurant and slapped him.

American Wit

No man's life, liberty, or property

are safe while

the legislature is in session.

—MARK TWAIN

Kilroy Was Here

*His most daring appearance was in the bathroom
reserved for President Harry Truman, Josef Stalin, and
Prime Minister Clement Atlee during the "Big Three"
conference in Potsdam, Germany, in July 1945. An
agitated Stalin returned from the bathroom and asked his
translator, "Who is Kilroy?" Wouldn't we all like to know?*

WHO IS KILROY? World War II's best-known GI didn't
earn any medals or carry a weapon, but he did get around.
The simple graffiti cartoon of a bald man with a long nose
peeking over a wall (sometimes gripping the wall with his
fingertips) and accompanied by the words "Kilroy was here"
has been spotted everywhere from the Statue of Liberty to
Hitler's Eagles' Nest retreat. For whatever reason—maybe
because they liked the idea that one of them was always
ahead of the enemy—something about Kilroy appealed to
American GIs. So they left his imprint everywhere.

BUT WHERE DID HE BEGIN? There are plenty of stories to
explain Kilroy's existence. At least 62 men with the surname
Kilroy served in the military during World War II, and at
least one—Sergeant Francis J. Kilroy Jr.—claims to be the
cartoon's inspiration, but his story couldn't be corroborated.
There's a rumor that the real Kilroy went AWOL and his
friends drew the cartoons in various places to throw off
military police. There's the popular but implausible theory

that the Kilroy cartoons were a secret agent's means of communicating with other spies. It's also unlikely that Kilroy was a copycat of a similar British graffito from the 1930s called Mr. Chad.

(How would American GIs be familiar with the old British cartoon, and why change his name?)

The most widely accepted origin is a real live Kilroy from Halifax, Massachusetts. James J. Kilroy inspected riveting work at the Fore River Shipyard in Quincy, marking each riveted section with a checkmark. Because welders were paid by the number of approved—and marked—sections, some began erasing the checkmark after approval, hoping to get a second payment. Kilroy began marking his sections "Kilroy was here," which couldn't be erased without being noticed. Months later, sailors doing repairs halfway around the world would find "Kilroy was here" in an inaccessible or sealed compartment. In 1946, during a radio contest investigating Kilroy's origins, Fore River workers corroborated Mr. Kilroy's claims about his unique inspection mark.

IS KILROY STILL LEAVING HIS MARK? Kilroy continued to show up after World War II and during the Korean War. As time passed, Kilroy became a rarity but didn't go extinct, even being seen recently in Iraq and Afghanistan.

Politics Is for the Dogs

CANDIDATE: Duke, a seven-year-old Great Pyrenees dog living in Cormorant, Minnesota

RUNNING FOR: Mayor of Cormorant

CAMPAIGN NOTES: Cormorant is a small township, and the mayor's job is purely ceremonial. That probably had a lot to do with David Rick, a resident of the township, entering his dog Duke in the mayor's race in 2014. How small is Cormorant? So small that only about a dozen people voted in the election . . . and at least seven of them voted for Duke—enough votes for him to beat his human opponent, Richard Sherbrook, and become mayor. Sherbrook says that even he voted for the hound after deciding it would be "pretty cool" to have a dog as mayor. "There's no question that he'll do a good job representing the community," Sherbrook told ABC News. "He's a sportsman and he likes to hunt. He'll really protect the town." (Cormorant holds mayoral elections every year, and Duke won reelection in 2015, 2016, and 2017.)

STRANGE TRIP

INJURED FOOT MONUMENT

LOCATION: Stillwater, New York

DETAILS: This headstone, about five feet tall with the sculpted likeness of a boot on it, is a memorial to America's most famous traitor—Benedict Arnold, the general who fought for the Americans during the Revolutionary War, then switched sides and sold secrets to the British. It was erected in 1887 in recognition of wounds Arnold received to his foot and leg while fighting for the American side—before he turned traitor—in the pivotal Battle of Saratoga in 1777. The memorial, which sits near where Arnold was injured in what is now Saratoga National Historic Park, was donated to the site by Revolutionary War historian and former Civil War general John Watts de Peyster. An inscription on the back of the memorial says it was erected for "the 'most brilliant soldier' of the Continental Army, who was desperately wounded on this spot" . . . but it doesn't mention Arnold's name—at all. It's the only American war monument dedicated to a specific soldier that doesn't bear that soldier's name.

REGIONAL TREAT

HORSESHOE SANDWICH

FOUND IN: Springfield, Illinois

DESCRIPTION: It's an open-faced sandwich of thick sourdough toast topped with ham, french fries, and a cheese sauce. It was invented at the Leland Hotel in 1928 by cooks Joe Schweska and Steve Tomko. Local legend says it was created to honor local horseshoe makers who frequently dined at the Leland. It was originally served on a hot metal platter (to represent an anvil); the ham looked like a horseshoe, and the fries resembled nails.

NASCAR Superstitions

DON'T DRIVE A GREEN CAR

Just a few months after winning the Indianapolis 500 in 1920, Gaston Chevrolet died after crashing into a car he didn't see. His car had been painted green, so from then on it was considered bad luck to drive a green car. (Very few drivers went with green for decades, until 1952, when Larry Mann crashed his green Hudson Hornet into a wall . . . and died.)

DON'T EAT PEANUTS IN THE STANDS

In the early days of NASCAR (before World War II), most races were held at local fairgrounds, and pit crews were stationed in the shade, right underneath the grandstands. Fans sat up there and ate peanuts, and dropped shells into the pits . . . and the cars. Wrecks at these races almost always had evidence of peanut shells, leading to the idea that peanuts were a bringer of doom.

DON'T SHAVE BEFORE A RACE

NASCAR driver Doc MacKenzie got married in 1936 and shaved off his long beard for the ceremony. On his first race afterward, at the Wisconsin State Fair, he crashed his

car and died. Fellow driver Ted Horn later quipped, "Doc shouldn't have shaved. That jinxed him."

DON'T DRESS YOUR LEFT SIDE FIRST

Many NASCAR drivers past and present believe that the right side is luckier than the left side, so that's how they dress on game day: underwear, pants, socks, shirt sleeves, and gloves all go on the right appendage before the left.

DON'T USE NO. 13

The number 13—in NASCAR as in so many places—is considered unlucky. It was rarely used as a car number until former Miami Dolphins quarterback Dan Marino became a team co-owner, and insisted his car use his old jersey number: 13. (In the 400 or so races where a 13 car has raced, it has finished in the top five only eight times.)

DON'T HANDLE $50 BILLS ON RACE DAY

Racer Joe Weatherly was killed at Riverside Raceway in California in 1964. Among his personal effects, two $50 bills were reportedly found in his pocket. Racers and crews have avoided fifties ever since.

WALK OF FAME

On February 9, 1960, actress Joanne Woodward was awarded the very first star on the Hollywood Walk of Fame—a stretch of 15 blocks along Hollywood Boulevard and three blocks along Vine Street. Since then, more than 2,600 stars have been molded into this stretch of sidewalk, honoring pioneers in film, TV, music, radio, and theater. But there's no such thing as a free lunch, or a free star . . . the cost of a Walk of Fame ceremony is $50,000. Celebrities may be nominated after death, and need not be real: Lassie, Mickey Mouse, and Godzilla are just a few of the fictional characters who have been honored.

AMERICA'S STRANGEST RACES

Big Dog's Backyard Ultra

"It's like being punched in the face. Not hard, just a little bit. But you do it again, and again, and again. Eventually you start to flinch when you see the punch coming." That's how Gary Cantrell describes this ultramarathon—named for his bulldog—that he invented on his land in Bell Buckle, Tennessee. The wooded track is 4.16666 miles, the distance an average runner should complete in an hour. Run a lap, rest until the hour is up. Run another lap, rest until the hour is up. Do it again, and again, and again . . .

There is no finish. A runner is disqualified if they fail to complete a lap in 60 minutes, or when they quit. The winner is the last runner standing.

It's as taxing mentally as it is physically. After a day or so, "You need somebody to tell you what to do," runner Dave Proctor told BBC Sport. "Eat this, drink this, go to the bathroom, and don't forget to wipe your bum." The current record belongs to Karel Sabbe, a Belgian dentist who ran 312.5 miles in a little over three days in 2020.

IT'S ANOTHER CONSPIRACY!

Americans actually believed this?
Yep!

THEORY: As a prisoner of war during the Vietnam War, Senator John McCain was brainwashed by the Viet Cong. They could "flip the switch" in his brain and turn him into a spy, or worse . . . anytime they wanted!

THE STORY: McCain, a US Navy pilot, was shot down over Saigon in 1967 and was held captive in a military prison for six years, subject to physical and psychological torture. The Vietnamese hypnotized him, brainwashed him, and implanted a chip in his brain. McCain was released in 1973, but the Vietnamese used the chip to force him to run for the US Senate and eventually president. As president, McCain would have been the helpless puppet of the communist government of Vietnam.

THE TRUTH: Sound familiar? It's the plot of the book (and movie) *The Manchurian Candidate*—conspiracy theorists just modernized it by adding

"the chip," which they borrowed from UFO
conspiracy theories. The theory probably stems
from McCain's controversial efforts to normalize
diplomatic relations with Vietnam in the 1980s.
This enraged many veterans and POWs, who
felt that Vietnam was still the enemy. From there
the rumors took off, first turning McCain into a
collaborator and then into someone with a chip
in his head. The story gained traction during his
unsuccessful presidential run in 2008.

Similar charges arose when Barack Obama took
office; he was accused of—either knowingly or
unknowingly—being a Manchurian Candidate for
the Muslim Brotherhood (who brainwashed him as
a child in Kenya).

WELCOME TO CURLY

*More Spanish city names,
and their English translations.*

CITY: Chino, California
MEANING: "Curly"

CITY: Escondido, California
MEANING: "Hidden"

CITY: Las Vegas, Nevada
MEANING: "The Meadows"

CITY: Fresno, California
MEANING: "Ash Tree"

CITY: Salinas, California
MEANING: "Salt Marsh"

CITY: Reno, Nevada
MEANING: "Reindeer"

Mar-a-Lago

When the Post Cereal heiress Marjorie Merriweather
Post died in 1973, she bequeathed Mar-a-Lago (Spanish
for "Sea-to-Lake"), her Florida estate, to the federal
government for use as a site for state visits by foreign
dignitaries or a winter White House for US presidents.
She also left a sum of money to provide for the upkeep of
the estate, but it wasn't enough to cover the actual costs of
running the place. President Richard Nixon helicoptered
in to look at it about a week before he resigned from office
in August 1974, but neither he nor President Jimmy
Carter were interested in using it. In 1981, Congress
passed legislation to return Mar-a-Lago to the Post estate.
Donald Trump bought it from the estate in 1985 . . . and
turned it into his winter White House after he was elected
president in 2016.

POLITICIANS **SPEAK**

A billion here, a billion there,
sooner or later it adds up
to real money.

—Everett Dirksen (R-IL)

SECRETS OF THE SUPER-CENTENARIANS

There's only about a 1 in 1,000 chance that a 100-year-old person will become a "super-centenarian"— live to see their 110th birthday. How did these long-lived Americans make it that far?

BESSE COOPER, MONROE, GEORGIA (116)

"I mind my own business and I don't eat junk food."

SUSANNAH MUSHATT JONES, BROOKLYN, NEW YORK (116)

Jones, who died in May 2016, never had children, slept 10 hours a night, and ate four strips of bacon every day at breakfast. "I never drink or smoke. I surround myself with love and positive energy. That's the key to long life and happiness."

BERNICE MADIGAN, CHESHIRE, MASSACHUSETTS (115)

"No children, no stress, and a spoonful of honey every day." Madigan also ate her favorite breakfast—Eggo waffles smothered in banana slices, and four glazed donut holes—daily.

GERTRUDE WEAVER, CAMDEN, ARKANSAS (116)

"Trusting in the Lord, hard work, and love everybody . . . Just do what you can, and if you can't, you can't."

BENJAMIN HARRISON HOLCOMB, CARNEGIE, OKLAHOMA (111)

Big breakfasts and small dinners. "All his life, Daddy didn't smoke, he didn't drink. But he did have a huge breakfast. Just huge. Eggs, sausage. And just cornmeal mush for dinner," Holcomb's daughter, Leola Ford, told the *Washington Times* in 2000.

LEILA DENMARK, ATHENS, GEORGIA (114)

Denmark was the world's oldest practicing pediatrician when she retired at the age of 103; by then she was treating the great-grandchildren of her first patients. (Her other claim to fame: codeveloping the whooping cough vaccine in the 1930s.) Denmark avoided milk, fruit juice, junk food, and sweets—including her many birthday cakes, because they contained sugar, which she hadn't eaten in 70 years. She drank only water.

GERTRUDE BAINES, LOS ANGELES, CALIFORNIA (115)

Ate plenty of bacon, fried chicken, and ice cream, but "she never did drink, she never did smoke, and she never did fool around."

A BISON BY ANY OTHER NAME . . .

A herd of bison roaming the plain is an iconic image of the American frontier—so iconic, in fact, that the American bison was declared the country's national mammal in 2016. The animal's scientific name is *Bison bison bison*, but it's fine to refer to them simply as "bison." Just don't call them buffalo: though the two species are distantly related genetically, the only true buffaloes are the Asian water buffalo, which lives

in southeast Asia, and the African buffalo, found in sub-Saharan Africa. (Historians believe the use of "buffalo" among early settlers may have come from *boeuf*, the French word for "beef.")

The American bison is the largest land mammal in North America and one of the largest types of wild cattle in the world. An adult male bison is 6 feet tall and between 10 and 12 feet long; baby bison, nicknamed "red dogs" because of their reddish hair, can weigh up to 70 pounds at birth. And that big hump on a bison's back isn't just for looks: it's a combination of vertebrae and muscles that allow an animal to essentially use its head as a snowplow during winter weather.

AMERICA:
HOME OF THE
WORLD'S LARGEST . . .
PRAIRIE CHICKEN

LOCATION: Rothsay, Minnesota

DETAILS: Once home to the state's largest population of prairie chickens, Rothsay is now home to the world's largest single prairie chicken, a cement-and-steel bird built by a onetime trucker named Art Fosse. Though his name implies otherwise, Art never considered himself a true artist, just a guy who's good with a blowtorch. The bird he built back in the 1970s stands 13 feet tall and weighs 9,000 pounds. In case you're counting, that's about 8,998 pounds more than a real prairie chicken.

THE BOSS SINGS NEW JERSEY

It goes without saying that Bruce Springsteen is one of the nation's songwriting icons, and his catalog is an essential part of Americana. While the stories in many of his songs could take place anywhere, though, he's devoted to crooning about his home state of New Jersey (his very first album is *Greetings from Asbury Park, NJ*, after all). Here's a small sampling of the Boss's New Jersey–centric tunes.

"ATLANTIC CITY"

"THE E STREET SHUFFLE"

"4TH OF JULY, ASBURY PARK (SANDY)"

"IN FREEHOLD"

"TENTH AVENUE FREEZE-OUT"

"JERSEY GIRL"

If Anything Can Go Wrong...

Every American has had a run-in with the law...
Murphy's Law, that is. But where did the
concept come from?

Edwards Air Force Base, in California's Mojave Desert, opened its Flight Test Center during World War II as a place to research, develop, and test aerospace systems for the US military. In 1949, Captain John Paul Stapp was the lead on a project to test how the g-force (the force of gravity acting on the body at sea level) affected pilots during plane crashes, and how much g-force they could tolerate. To simulate the force of crashes, Stapp acted as his own guinea pig and rode in a rocket-powered sled named the *Gee Whiz* that accelerated to speeds of about 200 miles per hour and then slammed to a stop. An engineer named Captain Edward A. Murphy Jr. arrived at the base with sensors that he called "strain gauges." Murphy's sensors could measure the g-force on various parts of Stapp's body when he rode the *Gee Whiz*. However, the sensors were wired wrong during one test run, thus producing data that was incorrect.

Over the years, there have been differing accounts about Murphy's reaction, but most people agree that he grumbled about the installation technicians, saying, "If there's any way they can do it wrong, they will." As Murphy's complaint made its way around the base, it became, "If anything can go wrong, it will," the basic principle of Murphy's Law. The first time the public heard the phrase was at a press conference a few weeks later, when Stapp praised the project's engineers for their good safety record. A belief in what they were all now calling "Murphy's Law," Stapp claimed, made them work to eliminate any possible problems.

What's a Mermaid Got to Do with It?

When Starbucks Coffee Tea and Spices opened in
Seattle in 1971, the founders named the company
after a character from the novel *Moby-Dick* and
wanted something associated with the sea for its
logo. They found a 16th-century wood carving of a
two-tailed mermaid, then hired graphic designer
Terry Heckler to build on that. His design was a
crowned, naked mermaid . . . still with the two tails.
In 1987, after Starbucks was acquired by Howard
Schultz and began a national expansion, the decision
was made to lose the mermaid's lower half (and her
navel), cut out most of the tail (the rest is off to the
sides and looks like arms now), and to focus on her
smiling face.

Too Clever for Words

The New York Times *crossword puzzle is an American institution, and has long been famous for its clever clues. Here are six of our favorites—the question mark in the prompt is a clue that the answer is a pun, and the number tells you how many letters are in the answer. Can you puzzle them out?*
For answers, turn to page 404.

1. **Northern hemisphere? (5)**

2. **Army threats? (6)**

3. **Pat on the buns? (4)**

4. **Life preserver? (3)**

5. **Jam ingredients? (5)**

6. **Sentence structure? (4)**

Hiking Doll's Head Trail

Joel Slaton was bored in 2011. The Great Recession had cut deep into his carpentry business, and with his son off at college, the single dad started exploring the urban forests on the outskirts of Atlanta, where he grew up. While hiking at Constitution Lakes Park, he picked up a lot of trash—or "found objects," like toys and car parts that had piled up after years of illegal dumping. With those objects, he crafted disturbing little art displays and scattered them along the 2.5-mile trail. One day, he found the head of a doll, and the phrase "Doll's Head Trail" just "popped in my head and wouldn't go away."

Today, Doll's Head Trail is included on Atlanta's official tourism maps, and it's as creepy as it sounds. Like a bad omen in a horror movie, hikers round a bend and come face-to-face with a dirty, eyeless doll head that has a body made of sticks, *Blair Witch* style. If you hike this trail, you're welcome to create your own morbid display, but it has to consist of stuff you found in the area (and no stealing from other displays). As for Slaton, he's proud of his strange creation: "It has an air of mischief and mystery!"

CHEESY ORIGINS

Who made the first Philly cheesesteak? It depends on who you ask. In 1930, Pasquale "Pat" Olivieri was a hot dog vendor in South Philadelphia. One day, he put some beef on his grill next to the frankfurters, and a passing cabbie, lured by the aroma, asked for a steak sandwich. Soon, cabbies from around the city were stopping by Pat's cart for the sandwiches. The sandwiches became so popular that Pat opened a restaurant—Pat's King of Steaks—on Passyunk Avenue. It's still around, grilling 24 hours a day. Story number two comes from Joe Vento, founder of Geno's Steaks, which opened across the street from Pat's in 1966. Pat may have been the first to put steak on a bun, but Vento claims that he was the first to put cheese in the sandwich, thereby inventing the cheesesteak.

Either way, the two restaurants have been competing for the title of best cheesesteak ever since. Both Joe Vento and Frank Olivieri (Pat's current owner and the founder's nephew) claim that theirs is the superior sandwich . . . even though neither has actually tried his competition.

WHERE ROUTE 66 MEETS JURASSIC PARK

Holbrook, Arizona, looks like any other middle-of-nowhere desert town . . . aside from all the dinosaurs. Made of cement and painted in bright colors, there are two outside a shop called Rocks on Route 66, and another one looming behind the Chamber of Commerce. There are eight more dinosaurs in the parking lot of Jim Gray's Petrified Wood Co., and seven more at the Rainbow Rock Shop. The largest one there (perhaps it's a brontosaurus? They're not the most scientifically accurate . . .) is bright green and 25 feet tall. Another one (a T. rex, maybe?) has a cement snake in its jaws. There's even a cement baby dinosaur hatching from a cement egg.

Most of these dinosaurs once inhabited nearby highways, but after the attractions they were promoting closed in 2007, they took over the town. And the Rainbow Rock Shop owners have

been adding new ones of their own.

Holbrook is no stranger to dinosaurs: Gertie the Dinosaur was discovered at Petrified Forest National Park in 1985. Named after the dinosaur character in the 1914 animated short of the same name, this 225-million-year-old *Chindesaurus* fossil is one of many fossils that have been dug up in these parts.

Another fun fact? Holbrook was the inspiration for the animated film *Cars*.

Nice to Meat You

Carl Sagan once said, "If you wish to make an apple pie from scratch, you must first invent the universe." In that sense, Andy George of Minnesota may not have made his chicken sandwich completely from scratch (because he didn't invent the universe), but he came pretty close. For his *How to Make Everything* YouTube channel, George gave himself the challenge of making every ingredient in a chicken sandwich. It only took him six months and cost about $1,500. First step: he grew the vegetables (for toppings) and wheat (for the bread). Then he traveled to the sea and desalinated ocean water to get the salt. He milked a cow to make the butter and the cheese, which he churned and whipped by hand. He collected honey from a beehive for the bread, and then ground the wheat to make the dough. Six months later, he had all of the ingredients except one: the bird. He went to a farm, slaughtered a chicken, defeathered it, butchered it, cooked it, and then combined the meat with the bread and toppings. And then he ate his $1,500 sandwich. His reaction: "It's not bad."

STRANGEST LAWS

* In Devon, Colorado, it's illegal to walk backward after sunset.

* In Connecticut, it's against the law to play Scrabble while waiting for a politician to speak.

* Eating soup with a fork is against the law in New York.

* It's illegal to sell used confetti in Detroit.

THE ONLY PRESIDENT TO …

THE PRESIDENT: Abraham Lincoln

NOTABLE ACHIEVEMENT: Only president to earn a patent. In 1849, Lincoln invented a type of buoy. Lincoln is also the only US president to have worked as a bartender.

THE PRESIDENT: Grover Cleveland

NOTABLE ACHIEVEMENT: Only president to get married in the White House. A bachelor when he was elected, the 49-year-old president married 21-year-old Frances Folsom on June 2, 1886, in a small ceremony in the Blue Room. The marriage lasted until his death in 1908; in 1913, Rose became the first presidential widow to remarry.

THE PRESIDENT: Theodore Roosevelt

NOTABLE ACHIEVEMENT: Only president to be blind in one eye. Roosevelt took a hard punch to his left eye in a boxing match. It actually detached the retina, leaving Roosevelt blind in his left eye for the rest of his life. The boxing match occurred in 1908, while Roosevelt was president.

THE PRESIDENTS: George H. W. Bush and George W. Bush

NOTABLE ACHIEVEMENT: The Bushes are not the only father and son who both served in the Oval Office (the Adamses did as well), but they're the only father-son presidents who were fighter pilots in their younger days.

THE PRESIDENT: Gerald Ford

NOTABLE ACHIEVEMENT: Only president to survive two assassination attempts in the same month. In September 1975, former Charles Manson follower Lynette "Squeaky" Fromme tried to shoot Ford when he reached out to shake her hand in a public meet-and-greet. She pulled the trigger, but the gun's chamber was empty. Just three weeks later another woman, Sara Jane Moore, fired on Ford in a similar crowd situation, but a bystander knocked her arm away.

FIVE FREAKY FACTS ABOUT ...
US HOLIDAYS

✱ Roughly 15,600 Americans went to the emergency room for Fourth of July fireworks mishaps in 2020—up by more than 5,000 from 2019.

✱ If you like jack-o'-lanterns, head to Keene, New Hampshire, next Halloween. Every year they break their own world record for the most lit jack-o'-lanterns on display. (Their current record: 30,581.)

✱ The average trick-or-treater eats about 7,000 calories of candy on Halloween, totaling 675 grams of sugar. That's the equivalent of eating 169 sugar cubes.

✱ An estimated 46 million turkeys end up on Americans' Thanksgiving dinner tables annually. With 328 million Americans, that comes out to one turkey for every seven people.

✱ 'Twas the week before Christmas in 1965 . . . NASA astronauts Tom Stafford and Wally Schirra had smuggled a harmonica and some actual jingle bells onto the Gemini 6A spaceflight. They delivered a rousing rendition of "Jingle Bells," the first song broadcast from space.

What a Humdinger!

South Dakota's Jewel Cave is 137 miles long, the second-longest cave system in the world. The national monument's name comes from the sparkling calcite crystals that miners and brothers Frank and Albert Michaud discovered when they first explored the cave in 1900. But in addition to the crystals, one of the cave's most interesting features is the strong wind that often blows through its passages. These winds are caused by changes in barometric pressure, even in places that are miles from the cave entrance. Sections of the cave where the wind is exceptionally strong or loud have names like Hurricane Corner, Whistle Stop, Exhaust Pipe, Humdinger, and Drafty Maneuver.

POLITICIANS

SPEAK

Always be sincere,

even if you don't

mean it.

—HARRY S. TRUMAN

MICHIGAN MOTORING FIRSTS

* Detroit had the first mile (Woodward Avenue between 6 and 7 Mile roads) of concrete highway in the world in 1909.

* The first drive-in gas station opened in 1910 in Detroit.

* The nation's first painted center lines (on River Road near Trenton) were drawn in 1911.

* The nation's first roadside park (on US Route 2, Iron County) was opened in 1919, and first roadside picnic tables (US Route 16, Ionia) were constructed in 1929.

* The first state welcome center was opened in 1935 near Buffalo.

* Packard Motor Car Company introduced the first automobile air conditioning in 1939.

* The first urban freeway—the Davison Freeway in Detroit—was completed in 1942.

NUCLEAR OOPS

On May 22, 1957, a US Air Force B-36 was in flight, carrying one of the most powerful thermonuclear weapons ever made by the United States: a 10-megaton Mark-17 hydrogen bomb. During the flight, a single locking pin was used to secure the bomb and prevent it from being accidentally dropped by the plane. But the pin was removed for takeoffs and landings (so the bomb could be jettisoned in an emergency). On that morning, the B-36 was on its final approach to New Mexico's Kirtland Air Force Base when—according to one version of events—crew member First Lieutenant Bob Carp had just finished removing the locking pin when the plane hit turbulence and Carp lost his balance. He reached for the nearest thing he could grab to steady himself—the manual release lever for the bomb—and pulled it. With the locking pin removed, the bomb slipped from the bomb rack, crashed through the bomb bay doors, and fell to the earth some 2,000 feet below. (Carp claimed a snagged safety line was to blame for releasing the bomb.) The plutonium capsule was removed from the bomb at the time, so there was no danger of a nuclear explosion. But the TNT did detonate

when the bomb hit the ground, creating a crater 12 feet deep and 25 feet across, and killing a cow. The force of the blast was enough that pieces of the bomb (and the cow) were found more than a mile away.

Ten months later, on March 11, 1958, an unarmed 30-kiloton atom bomb fell from a US Air Force B-47. The locking pin was jammed in an unlocked position and crew member Bruce Kulka was sent to the bomb bay to insert the pin by hand. Kulka was a navigator, not a bombardier, and no idea where the pin was. While looking for it, he tried to pull himself up onto the bomb . . . by yanking on a handle that turned out to be the manual release lever. The bomb crashed through the bomb doors and fell some 15,000 feet, landing in the Mars Bluff, South Carolina, yard of Walter Gregg. The bomb's TNT detonated on impact, destroying Gregg's home and leaving a 30-foot-deep crater where his garden had been. (Luckily the only casualties were three of the Gregg family's chickens.) The government paid Gregg $54,000 for his troubles, and the air force ordered that nuclear bombs remain locked in their bomb racks during all future takeoffs and landings. (About time.)

A CITY OF SUPERLATIVES,
PART IV

The Big Apple isn't the only big-city nickname.
For instance, there's . . .

HOUSTON, THE MAGNOLIA CITY: First coined in the 1870s. Parts of the city occupy what used to be large forests of magnolia trees.

NEW ORLEANS, THE BIG EASY: There are two versions of this nickname's origins, both from the early 1900s. Theory #1: Musicians called it "the Big Easy" because it was so easy to find work in one of the city's many nightclubs. Theory #2: There were too few cops in New Orleans to enforce Prohibition, so there were a lot of illegal bars—so many that the city earned the nickname the "Big Speakeasy," or the "Big Easy," for short.

The White House Is for the Birds

Presidential dogs and cats get a lot of press (some with more favorable coverage than their owners). But did you know about these presidential birds?

- ★ Zachary Taylor's canary, Johnny Ty, died when the family brought him a mate. They thought they found him a lovebird, but it turned out that both birds were males. Oops!

- ★ Among the presidents who kept parrots, Teddy Roosevelt had a macaw named Eli Yale. Dolley Madison, wife of James Madison, liked to stroll the White House grounds with her green parrot perched on her shoulder.

- ★ President Kennedy's children had two parakeets: Bluebelle and Marybelle. Daughter Caroline also raised ducklings (though they didn't get along with the family's Welsh terrier, Charlie).

- ★ The Coolidges had a virtual aviary: three canaries, a thrush, a mockingbird, and a goose named Enoch.

- ★ James Buchanan had probably the most fitting pets for an American president: a pair of bald eagles.

The Fight over Flight

The Wright brothers were from Ohio but made their first successful flight in North Carolina, so both states try to claim the duo as their own. Over the years, a détente has evolved with Ohio being recognized as the place where the brothers lived and developed their inventions and North Carolina being the site of their first flight. To document this, both states print an homage to the Wrights on their license plates: Ohio includes the slogan "Birthplace of Aviation Pioneers" or "Birthplace of Aviation," and North Carolina's is "First in Flight." Also, both Ohio and North Carolina use an image of the Wright brothers' glider *Flyer I* on their state quarters.

Chief Seattle's Speech?

It is the most stirring and oft-quoted of native American speeches, supposedly delivered by Chief Seattle in 1854. In it he refers to the earth as his mother and the rivers as the blood of his ancestors. He also expresses his grief at having seen "a thousand rotting buffaloes on the prairie, left by the white men who shot them from a passing train."

Yet these words were never spoken by that famous chief. They were, in fact, the invention of a Hollywood screenwriter by the name of Ted Parry who gave them to a Seattle-like character in the 1972 movie *Home*. Since then, millions of people have associated the speech with the real Seattle.

Continuing Adventures of Florida Man

WRITTEN ON HIS FACE

The prominent Florida tattoo on the face of 22-year-old Matthew Leatham was the first indicator he's a true Florida Man. Leatham solidified that status by calling 9-1-1 numerous times one night in February 2021 and demanding that police give him a ride home. When the Pasco County dispatcher said they

don't do that, Leatham reportedly swore at them. He was cited for possession of marijuana, misusing the emergency 9-1-1 system, and for having a giant tattoo of Florida on his forehead.

Elsie the Cow:
A New Jersey Jersey Cow

A Jersey cow from New Jersey named You'll Do Lobelia was christened the Borden dairy company's first official Elsie in 1939 at the New York World's Fair. The newly dubbed Elsie went on to become one of the world's most famous mascots; she appeared in movies and even toured cross-country in her car, the Cowdillac. Sadly, after being seriously injured in a traffic accident in 1941, the first Elsie returned to her home at the Gordon-Walker Farm in Plainsboro, where she was put to sleep and buried under a headstone that reads, "A Pure Bred Jersey Cow. One of the Great Elsies of Our Time."

American Wit

The best way to teach your kids

about taxes is by

eating 30 percent of

their ice cream.

—BILL MURRAY

THE HIGHEST COURT IN THE LAND

Bet you didn't know that there's a basketball court in the Supreme Court Building. It's on the fifth (and top) floor, which was originally designed for storage; it was converted into a gym in the 1940s, and, later, the basketball court was added. It's smaller than regulation, but any employee can use it: security guards, clerks, off-duty police, cafeteria workers, and the justices themselves get involved in pickup games and tournaments. Just not during working hours—a sign by the entrance clearly states, "Playing basketball and weightlifting are prohibited while court is in session."

You. Lottery. Loser.

Nick Lynough, 22, of Elmira, New York, was "offended" by a state lottery ticket that he claims insulted him personally. The $5 ticket, which he purchased from a lottery machine at an inn, featured a game in which you rub off three random words, a "Person," a "Place," and a "Thing." (The player wins a prize if any of the words revealed matches the ones printed at the top of the ticket.) Lynough's ticket wasn't a winner, and adding insult to injury were the three words he got: "You," "Elmira," "Trash." After complaining to the New York State Gaming Commission, he was assured that the ticket was real. The commission decided to remove the word "Trash" from future tickets, and reassured Lynough that "the unfortunate arrangement of words on this individual ticket was completely random, coincidental and—most importantly—unintentional." They added that Lynough's losing ticket is actually quite special: "There was a 1 in 900 million chance of the words appearing in that order—meaning players would have a better chance of winning the Powerball or Mega Millions drawings than finding that phrase." Lynough still isn't convinced that makes him a winner.

STRANGE PLACES TO SPEND THE NIGHT

THE SIDE OF A CLIFF

LOCATION: Kent Mountain Adventure Center in Estes Park, Colorado

DETAILS: Talk about a Rocky Mountain high! First, you're guided up a steep trail to the top of a sheer cliff with breathtaking views. Then you're strapped into a harness, and you rappel down to a spot on the cliffside hundreds of feet above the ground. There, you're tied to a securely attached "sky cot," where you'll be fed dinner before enjoying the sunset. Then you settle in for the night. When you awake (if you slept), you're served breakfast, and then you rappel the rest of the way down. This "leisure" activity was invented out of necessity when rock climbers needed more than one day to complete their climbs.

BE SURE TO . . . use the bathroom at the base. Otherwise, you either have to hold it until the morning, or rappel down early (which takes 30 minutes). Or, you can do your business under the stars into the provided 3-ply trash bag full of chemicals that turn your business into a gel. "The bags work pretty well if that's needed," said Dustin Dyer, co-owner of Kent Mountain, "which isn't very often." (Translation: most people hold it.)

Me Politician I Talk Good

Who am I? Why am I here?
—Adm. James Stockdale,
at a vice presidential debate in 1992

The number one job facing the middle class, and it happens to be a three-letter word: J-O-B-S.
—Joe Biden

Families is where our nation finds hope, where wings take dream.
—George W. Bush

We have a lot of kids who don't know what work means. They think work is a four-letter word.
—Hillary Clinton

I'm not a doctor. I'm like a person who has a good [points to his head] you know what.
—Donald Trump

Party Animals

DEMOCRAT DONKEY

Andrew Jackson's critics thought he was a jack . . . er, donkey. The slave-owning, Indian-displacing Democrat embraced that image—even though his Republican opponents were using it to deride him in the 1828 presidential election. Out of spite, Jackson added a donkey to his campaign posters. The image stuck with Old Hickory until his death in 1837. That year, a political cartoon called "A Modern Baalim and His Ass" (by a cartoonist whose name has been lost to history) was the first one to use a donkey to represent the entire Democratic Party. Then it faded from use.

The donkey symbol would have most likely died out completely had it not been resurrected 30 years later by Thomas Nast, an influential political cartoonist for *Harper's Weekly*. A liberal Republican, Nast used a menagerie of animals in his cartoons. For instance, Democrats also became foxes and two-headed tigers, but it was the donkey that the party would eventually adopt as its mascot . . . even though it was originally meant as an insult.

Johnny Apple Cider

Most of us know Johnny Appleseed—born John Chapman in 1774 in Massachusetts—as a cartoonlike figure, wearing an upturned pot for a hat and lovingly sowing apple orchards from Pennsylvania as far as Illinois during the early 19th century. The expert nurseryman anticipated where population was likely to swell and entered the area to cultivate apple trees that he could sell to incoming settlers. All in all, he was responsible for more than 100,000 square miles of orchards.

But Johnny's apples weren't like the sweet, edible varieties around today. The bitter fruit was used primarily for one thing: alcohol. Hard apple cider was a staple beverage on the American frontier, with the average settler drinking more than 10 ounces each day. This was partly because water could harbor dangerous bacteria, making cider a safe, reliable alternative.

So what transformed the apple from favorite boozy beverage to a daily snack? Prohibition.

THE SURPRISE PARTY

Gracie Allen (comedian and wife of George Burns) ran for president in 1940 on the Surprise Party ticket. The party's slogan: "Down with Common Sense!" Allen took that satirical message on a 34-city whistle-stop train tour along with her mascot, a kangaroo named Laura. Ever the innovative one, Allen claimed to have invented the sew-on campaign pin "so the voter can't change his mind." Like any good politician, she kissed babies, but refused to kiss male babies unless they were "over 21." Among her more memorable campaign promises was to make Congress work on commission. "When the country prospers," she speechified to the delighted crowds, "Congress would get 10 percent of the additional take." Of course, Allen didn't become president, but she was—surprise!—elected mayor of Monominee, Michigan (even though she wasn't on the ballot). Allen politely turned down the opportunity to serve as the town's mayor because she didn't live there.

GOVERNMENT (MIS)MANAGEMENT

In 2002, the General Accounting Office reported finding that at least 200 US Army personnel spent $38,000 on personal expenses using Defense Department–issued credit cards. According to reports, many of the charges (including "lap dancing") were made at strip clubs near military bases. Other charges: mortgage payments, racetrack betting, Internet gambling, and Elvis photos from Graceland. Further investigation revealed that many government offices abuse charge card programs. Some examples cited by the GAO: laptop computers, pet supplies, DVD players, pizzas, and $30,000 worth of Palm Pilots.

Ellis Island Mix-ups?

One enduring American misconception is that officials at Ellis Island often changed the names of immigrants because they couldn't pronounce or spell the foreign names. Although some immigrants undoubtedly changed their names when they entered the United States, most were not the result of ignorant Ellis Island employees. Ellis Island (now a national monument) employed hundreds of translators throughout the island's tenure as America's premier immigration station. The translators spoke Yiddish, Russian, Italian, Lithuanian, and many more languages. Most were either immigrants themselves or the children of immigrants and, thus, could easily converse with the new arrivals. Records and travel documents were also thoroughly inspected, and shipping companies, which were in charge of drawing up the documents, took great pains to make them accurate since immigrants whose documents were incomplete or incorrect were deported at the shipping company's expense.

THE GROUNDHOG, THE MYTH, THE LEGEND

We all know the Groundhog Day drill: On February 2 each year, a groundhog named Phil makes an appearance in Punxsutawney, Pennsylvania. If Phil sees his shadow, we'll have six more weeks of winter; no shadow, spring is sure to come early. But how much do you really know about America's celebrity marmot?

* Phil's official name is "Punxsutawney Phil, Seer of Seers, Sage of Sages, Prognosticator of Prognosticators, and Weather Prophet Extraordinaire."

* When he's not predicting the weather, Phil and his female companion, Phyllis, live in a climate-

controlled area called the Groundhog Zoo. It's a fiberglass enclosure connected to the Punxsutawney Memorial Library. There, he spends 364 days a year in leisure . . . mostly napping. A group of locals who call themselves the Inner Circle and have prestigious titles like "Stump Warden" and "Fair Weatherman" care for the couple.

* The Inner Circle claims that there's been only one Phil, and that he's more than 130 years old—according to legend, he stays fit by sipping "groundhog punch," which adds seven years to his life every time he takes a drink. No one knows for sure how many groundhogs have played the role over the years. But because a groundhog's average lifespan is six to eight years, a fair estimate is that there have been 15 or 20 Phils since 1886, when the first official Groundhog Day was celebrated.

* Once Phil decides whether or not spring will come early, he (supposedly) announces his prediction to the Inner Circle's president in a language called Groundhogese. The president translates for the rest of the world.

* The folks in Punxsutawney claim that Phil is always right with his weather predictions. Not so. According to weather records, he's correct only about 40 percent of the time.

FIVE FREAKY FACTS ABOUT ...
OHIO

* Columbus was home to America's first kindergarten (1838) and first junior high school (1909).

* "Hang on Sloopy" by the McCoys is the state's official rock song.

* Alcoholics Anonymous held their first meeting in Akron in 1935.

* The state has 19 species of native crayfish.

* Better put a lid on your pooch! Police officers in Paulding are allowed to bite a dog to silence it.

AMERICAN INNOVATION

In the early 1990s, Tim Derk was the guy inside the costume of the Coyote, the mascot for the San Antonio Spurs. Derk was responsible for coming up with his own stunts and routines; one of his most popular bits was using a foot-wide rubber band to fling Spurs T-shirts into the crowd. But it shot the shirts only a few rows up, and Derk thought the fans in the cheap seats were missing out, so he set out to create a version that could reach the upper decks. Derk and a friend (the guy inside the Phoenix Suns' gorilla costume) brainstormed ideas, and ultimately designed a prototype consisting of a four-foot-long cast-iron pipe outfitted with two carbon dioxide canisters. Derk got a mechanic to put the machine together, and used it for the first time at a Spurs game: he held it like a bazooka and shot shirts at the crowd while dressed up as "Rambote"—the Coyote in a Rambo outfit. The T-Shirt Cannon was born.

REGIONAL TREAT

HOT BROWN

FOUND IN: Louisville, Kentucky

DESCRIPTION: It's named after the place where it was created in 1926: the Brown Hotel. The most popular dish on the menu was ham and eggs, but chef Fred Schmidt became bored with making it. So he came up with this sandwich as an alternative: an open-faced sandwich of turkey, bacon, and Mornay sauce (a basic cheese sauce), cooked under a broiler. It quickly gained popularity because sliced turkey was a novelty at the time—it was rare to see turkey when it wasn't Thanksgiving. Result: within a year, the Hot Brown was being ordered by 95 percent of Brown Hotel customers.

PARANORMAL PARKS,
PART IV

America's national parks are full of ghostly tales…

THE AITU: NATIONAL PARK OF AMERICAN SAMOA

In Samoa, locals have long feared ghostly creatures called *aitu*, or evil spirits. The aitu are said to meet at the park's To'aga beach at noon and after sunset to frighten people who venture into their territory. When National Park Service officials started scouting the site during the early 1900s, Samoans warned them of the aitu, but one man—a pharmacist with the US Navy—learned about the spirits the hard way.

In 1924, while the pharmacist was living in Samoa, he encountered ghosts that continuously knocked on his front door; his wife had run-ins with similar spooks that wandered through the house and moved the furniture. And one evening, the pharmacist, his wife, and several other people encountered a party of headless revelers on To'aga beach. The pharmacist ultimately left the island, and the park offices were moved into town. But the threat of an aitu haunting remains, so if you're visiting Samoa, be sure to stay away from To'aga beach during prime aitu haunting hours!

Even More
Tax Dollars at Work

$ The National Institutes of Drug Abuse spent $780,000 and five years studying whether pizza is as addictive as drugs. Findings: 100 college students surveyed said they felt pizza is indeed addictive, but not as addictive as ice cream, chocolate, or french fries.

$ In 2015, the US Agency for International Development spent $2 million on a campaign urging Americans to visit Lebanon. That's the same year the State Department warned Americans to "avoid all travel in Lebanon because of ongoing safety and security concerns" because of ISIS terrorist cells operating inside the country.

$ NASA spent $1.2 million on a Colorado State University study of "the impact of space travel on bones." They simulated weightlessness by fitting two dozen sheep with braces that kept one hind leg in the air, throwing off their balance in a way that is only remotely similar to the loss of balance astronauts feel in zero gravity.

$ In an effort to reduce stress levels and improve the self-esteem of public housing tenants, the US Department of Housing and Urban Development spent $860,000 on a "Creative Wellness" program in 2001. The plan: the government paid to enhance the tenants' lifestyles through "aromatherapy, color therapy, and 'gemstone support.'"

POLITICAL THEATER

Film buff Jimmy Carter watched five movies a week during his presidency. The very first, screened at the White House two days after his 1977 inauguration: *All the President's Men*, the story of how *Washington Post* writers Bob Woodward and Carl Bernstein uncovered the Watergate scandal (which led to the resignation of his predecessor Richard Nixon).

POLITICIANS

SPEAK

I could have just
really unwound my whole
term as governor by launching
into a description of my
communing with the spirits.

—Rep. Tim Kaine (D-VA)

POISONING GENERAL WASHINGTON

Phoebe Fraunces, the daughter of a New York tavernkeeper, reportedly saved the life of General George Washington after pretending to sympathize with English spies. When Thomas Hickey, a member of Washington's guard, told her to serve the general a plate of poisoned peas, she did so, and then whispered a warning to Washington. He (or she, depending on which version you read) immediately flipped the peas out the window, where some chickens ate them and died. Hickey was later executed for treason.

An Alligator on Staten Island

In 2019, Kim Walker called 9-1-1 to report that she and her husband had just wrangled an alligator out of a patch of woods in New York City. The dispatcher didn't believe her. "I promise I'm not crazy," Kim pleaded. "I'm not stoned, not delusional. We just caught an alligator!" It was true. Her husband, Don, had come across the three-foot-long reptile while searching for fishing bait in the woods. Determined to wrangle it himself, he had two things going for him: "I've watched enough TV, plus I've lived in Florida."

Channeling the spirit of Steve Irwin, Don tossed some blood bait at the alligator to lure it close to him. Then? "I just dragged him up on land, got on top of him, held his head, and my wife taped his mouth shut and that was it." Presumed to be a lost pet, the alligator was named Charlie and turned over to wildlife rehabilitators. At last report, Charlie was living in Brooklyn. (Hopefully, he's staying out of the sewers.)

Emperor Norton

Joshua Norton was a wealthy 19th-century businessman and speculator who settled in San Francisco. In 1853, he bet his fortune on the rice market and lost it all; by 1856, he was completely bankrupt. The experience left him mentally deranged, his head filled with delusions that he was emperor of California. In 1859, Norton promoted himself to emperor of the United States, and when the Civil War seemed inevitable, he issued proclamations abolishing the US Congress and dissolving the republic, and assumed the powers of the American presidency.

No one listened, of course, but as the years passed, Californians—San Franciscans especially—began to treat Norton as if he really were an emperor: Riverboat companies and even the Central Pacific Railroad gave him lifetime free passes, and the state senate set aside a special seat for him in the senate chamber. Theaters admitted him without a ticket, and audiences showed their

deference by standing as the emperor entered the hall. He printed 25-cent and 50-cent banknotes . . . which were accepted by local businesses.

When the San Francisco police arrested him for lunacy, the judge dressed down the officers for detaining a man who "had shed no blood, robbed no one, and despoiled no country, which is more than can be said for most fellows in the king line."

Even city hall played along, picking up the tab for Norton's 50-cents-a-night "Imperial Palace" (a room in a boardinghouse) and buying him a new set of clothes from the prestigious Bullock and Jones tailors when Norton's "imperial wardrobe"—which consisted of old military uniforms combined with a collection of crazy hats—became tattered and worn.

When Emperor Norton died penniless in 1880 at the age of 61, a businessmen's club picked up the tab for his lavish imperial funeral. More than 10,000 people came to the viewing.

THE KITCHEN SINK

Want to try your luck at an eating challenge, but your tastes lean more sweet than savory? Try the Kitchen Sink Sundae Contest at San Francisco Creamery Co. in Walnut Creek, California. What goes into the Kitchen Sink? Three sliced bananas, eight scoops of ice cream, eight toppings, plus loads of whipped cream, toasted almonds, and cherries. The dessert is so large that it's served in a kitchen sink–sized bowl (complete with faucet) and normally serves six people. But anybody who finishes it off on their own within the allotted time receives free ice cream for a year (if they can still stomach it).

Party Animals

REPUBLICAN ELEPHANT

Although an elephant was first used in a cartoon to describe Republicans in 1860, it was Thomas Nast (responsible for the Democrats' donkey) who popularized that symbol. In 1874, he took issue with *New York Herald* editors who were running alarmist editorials that charged Republican president Ulysses S. Grant with "Caesarism." Rumors abounded that Grant would run for a third term in 1876, which, even though it was legal at the time, was severely frowned upon. (And the rumors were false.) Nast was a close friend of Grant's, so in the cartoon he depicted the *Herald* as an ass in lion's clothing who "roamed about in the forest and amused himself by frightening all the foolish animals." One of the frightened animals was an elephant, which Nash labeled "the Republican Vote." Nast and his contemporaries kept that image alive, as well as the Democrats' donkey. By 1900, both animals were firmly entrenched in American politics.

A Blockbuster Collapse

Blockbuster boasts one of the most spectacular rises—and falls—in the history of American business. They were the first large video-rental chain, with more than 9,000 stores from coast to coast at their peak in 2004. In the 1980s, before VCR owners could "make it a Blockbuster night," the vast majority of video rental stores were small mom-and-pop operations. But they couldn't keep up with the local Blockbuster, which offered a huge selection and was much more likely to have the big hit movies and new releases in stock on a Saturday night. Another feature of Blockbuster: exorbitant late fees, which customers hated, but what choice did they have? None . . . until cheaper, more convenient, video-rental-by-mail services like Netflix arrived in the late 1990s and $1-a-day rental kiosks like Redbox started popping up in the early 2000s. Vanquished, Blockbuster filed for bankruptcy protection in 2010, and Dish Network bought around 1,700 of its locations before closing them down over the next few years. Today, you can still make it a Blockbuster night in Bend, Oregon—that's the only independently owned and operated store bearing the Blockbuster name still in operation.

STRANGE TRIP
ODDPORIUM

LOCATION: Arden, Delaware

DETAILS: Arden is a storybook village outside of Wilmington designed a century ago by an eccentric sculptor. It hasn't changed much since. Arden natives Ken and Beth Schuler were childhood friends who bonded over their love of odd things . . . and then each other. After Ken lost his job in 2014, they opened Oddporium in a building that had been in Ken's family for 100 years. What began as an antique shop and also boasts a museum (which hosts movie nights and lectures from paranormal experts) has gained a cult following; as one reviewer writes, "Definitely a customer for life and probably the afterlife too."

So what can you find at the "Gallery of the Peculiar and the Bizarre"? "There are a variety of things," says Ken, "that appeal to what we like to call 'fellow weirdos.'" Things like:

A lamp made from a human spine

A lamp made from a cow femur

Lobotomy tools

Embalming fluid bottles

Quack medicine nostrums

Old X-rays and psychiatric records

Tarot cards

Ouija boards

A working Tesla coil

An electroshock therapy machine

19th-century "mourning pins"
with the original death photos

A human skeleton named Lizzy

A preserved Cyclops
pig named Amelia

GOOD FORTUNE

Despite their ubiquity at Chinese restaurants, fortune cookies are an American invention, and the man who first sold them in the United States was Japanese. Makoto Hagiwara of the Japanese Tea Garden in San Francisco's Golden Gate Park started offering fortune cookies in the early 1900s, and by 1915, they were massively popular locally. Hagiwara's cookies included little "thank-you" notes instead of wise sayings. The cookies moved south around 1918, when Chinese baker

George Jung, who later owned the Hong Kong Noodle Company, began serving them at his Los Angeles restaurant.

So who came up with the idea of putting the notes inside? No one's sure, but according to legend, in the 13th century, the Chinese began to hide notes inside small pastries called mooncakes. They were fighting the Mongolians at the time, and most Mongolians didn't like the taste of the mooncakes and so would ignore the treats . . . making them a perfect way to pass secret messages.

Smarter than the Average Berra

Yogi Berra—former New York Yankees catcher and Major League manager and coach—is just as famous for his tendency to mangle the English language as for his epic career. Here are some favorite Yogi-isms.

"A nickel ain't worth a dime anymore."

"Always go to other people's funerals—otherwise they won't come to yours."

"Baseball is ninety percent mental, and the other half is physical."

"Even Napoleon had his Watergate."

"He hits from both sides of the plate. He's amphibious."

"I never said most of the things I said."

"If the world was perfect, it wouldn't be."

"I'm not going to buy my kids an encyclopedia. Let them walk to school like I did."

"If people don't want to come out to the ballpark, nobody's gonna stop 'em."

"In theory, there is no difference between theory and practice. In practice, there is."

"The future ain't what it used to be."

"You can observe a lot by just watching."

"Nobody goes there anymore. It's too crowded."

AN UNUSUAL CHAPEL

In 1874, after his New Orleans parish was spared during a deadly yellow fever outbreak, Catholic priest Father Leonard Thevis built a small chapel; a cemetery for parishioners was built around it shortly afterward. Father Thevis named the church and cemetery in honor of Saint Roch (pronounced "rock"), whose name is invoked to help those afflicted during epidemics. Since its opening, people have visited the site to pray to the saint, and have left behind what are known as *ex-votos*—offerings left in gratitude for perceived help. The ex-votos left at St. Roch Cemetery include plaster casts of body parts (hands, arms, legs, feet, brains, livers, hearts) representing the body parts of people being prayed for, prosthetics (mostly legs and feet), leg braces from polio victims, sets of false teeth, tufts of human hair, glass eyes, and more. These relics can be found hanging from the walls and on tables and shelves in a small room inside the chapel. The remains of Father Thevis are there, too, buried beneath the floor.

MORE STRANGE STATE SYMBOLS

Here are a few more fun official symbols for US states.

ARKANSAS'S STATE BEVERAGE: Milk

DELAWARE'S STATE DESSERT: Peach Pie

KANSAS'S STATE RED WINE GRAPE: Chambourcin

MAINE'S STATE HERB: Wintergreen

MISSISSIPPI'S STATE SHELL: Oyster

MONTANA'S STATE FOSSIL: Duck-Billed Dinosaur

NEBRASKA'S STATE SOFT DRINK: Kool-Aid

NEW HAMPSHIRE'S STATE POULTRY: New Hampshire Red

NEW YORK'S STATE SNACK: Yogurt

NORTH DAKOTA'S STATE HORSE: Nokota Horse

SOUTH CAROLINA'S STATE CRAFT: Sweetgrass Basket Weaving

WASHINGTON'S STATE OYSTER: Olympia Oyster

WEST VIRGINIA'S STATE ROCK: Coal

WISCONSIN'S STATE PASTRY: Kringle

First Lady Firsts

FIRST TO LIVE IN THE WHITE HOUSE:
Abigail Adams (1797).

FIRST TO *NOT* LIVE IN THE WHITE HOUSE (AFTER ITS CONSTRUCTION):
Anna Harrison, wife of William Henry Harrison. She didn't accompany her husband to his inauguration in 1841 because she was ill. President Harrison died a month later, and his wife never set foot in the White House.

FIRST TO ENJOY INDOOR PLUMBING IN THE WHITE HOUSE:
Abigail Fillmore (1850).

FIRST TO BE RELATED TO HER HUSBAND BY BLOOD:
Eleanor Roosevelt was a fifth cousin, once removed, of Franklin Roosevelt.

FIRST TO BE MOTHER OF A FUTURE PRESIDENT:
Abigail Adams, wife of John Adams, and mother of John Quincy Adams. (Barbara Bush, wife of George H. W. Bush, was the second.)

FIRST TO SERVE IN A PRESIDENTIAL ADMINISTRATION:
Sarah Polk was the official secretary of
President James K. Polk (1845).

FIRST TO MAKE A CAMEO APPEARANCE ON A SITCOM:
Betty Ford was a guest star on an episode of
The Mary Tyler Moore Show in 1975.

FIRST TO HAVE HER OWN SECRET SERVICE AGENT:
Florence Harding (1921).

FIRST TO HAVE A MONUMENT ERECTED IN HER HONOR:
Lady Bird Johnson. In 1969, a grove in the Redwood
National Forest was named for her.

FIRST TO BE FOREIGN-BORN:
Louisa Adams (wife of John Quincy Adams) was born in
London in 1775. (Melania Trump—born in Novo Mesto,
Slovenia—was the second.)

FIRST TO HAVE HER OWN PRESS SECRETARY:
Jacqueline Kennedy. In 1962, Kennedy performed another
first: she was the first First Lady to receive an Emmy
Award, for a televised tour of the White House.

FIRST TO BE HONORED BY *OUTLAW BIKER* MAGAZINE:
In 1995, the publication named Barbara Bush
"First Lady of the Century."

DOGS OF WAR

NEMO

On December 4, 1966, 22-year-old US Air Force airman
Robert A. Throneberg and his German shepherd, Nemo,
were patrolling the perimeter of Tan Son Nhut Air Base in
Vietnam; the base had been under attack from mortar fire,
and Throneberg and Nemo were tasked with finding the
enemy. Nemo detected and attacked a group of Vietcong
infiltrators, which bought Throneberg enough time to
call for reinforcements before being shot. Even though
Nemo was also shot, he crawled over to his handler and
saved his life by covering Throneberg's wounded and
unconscious body with his own until help arrived. Nemo
lost an eye, and, after eight months recovering in Vietnam,
was rewarded with a permanent kennel retirement at
Lackland Air Force Base in San Antonio. He continued
to work as a recruiting dog until his death in December
1972. Few canines received the hero's welcome that Nemo
did: treated as surplus military equipment, only about 200
of the thousands of dogs sent to Vietnam were returned to
the US.

Gr-r-reat Marketing!

In 1952, American cereal giant Kellogg's developed a tasty new option called Sugar Frosted Flakes of Corn. Before it hit the shelves, Kellogg's asked Americans to vote for one of four candidates to serve as cartoon spokesperson: Katy the Kangaroo, Newt the Gnu, Elmo the Elephant, and Tony the Tiger. Katy and Tony initially tied, but the tiger's winning personality soon edged out the competition. In 1953, advertising agency executive Leo Burnett presented Tony as the cereal's one and only spokes-tiger.

Children's book illustrator Martin Provensen drew the original Tony, but the tiger has gone through a number of cosmetic updates through the years. Tony's trademark growl came courtesy of Thurl Ravenscroft, whose booming bass is also associated with the sneering theme "You're a Mean One, Mr. Grinch." In the 1970s, Kellogg's expanded Tony's presence, making him the spokes-toon for some short-lived cereal spinoffs; they also offered a public peek into Tony's private life, introducing his wife (Mrs. Tony), son (Tony Jr.), and daughter (Antoinette, who was "born" in 1974, the Chinese Year of the Tiger).

More than 70 years later, Tony shows no signs of slowing down, and is still offering his original opinion of Frosted Flakes: "They're gr-r-reat!"

Ben Franklin's Inventions

Everyone's heard the story about Benjamin Franklin flying a kite during a thunderstorm and proving that lightning and electricity are one and the same. But his discoveries and inventions didn't end there. Here are some other things invented by Franklin:

Bifocals

The lightning rod

The Franklin stove

A flexible catheter for his brother, who suffered from kidney stones

A chair with a reversible seat that could function as a stepladder

An odometer to measure postal routes

A "long arm" mechanical device to pluck books from high shelves

Swim fins

ABDUCTED IN PASCAGOULA

Lighthouse Park, on the banks of Mississippi's Pascagoula River, has one of the nation's strangest historical markers. It recounts the harrowing tale told by Charles Hickson and Calvin Parker: The two shipyard workers were fishing there one night in October 1973 when a nearly silent football-shaped ship flew up to them. Hovering outside it were three bulky but legless alien beings. They grabbed the men in their clawlike hands and levitated into the ship, where Hickson and Parker were examined by a "giant eye," then by a "big, ugly creature" that looked robotic. Then, as Parker remembered years later:

> This more feminine looking creature came out . . . She had regular fingers . . . and pinched me on the cheek, and then she took her finger and ran it down my throat and got it behind that thing that hangs down back there and tried to come up in my nasal cavity, and that's when it started hurting and I started choking and I got scared, and she

just kind of telepathically told me, "Don't be afraid, we aren't going to hurt you."

After about 30 minutes of this, Hickson and Parker were freed. They went to the police . . . who actually believed them. "We did everything we knew to try to break their stories," said Jackson County Sheriff's Captain Glen Ryder. "If they were lying to me, they should be in Hollywood." Even still, the close encounter haunted both men. Parker believes that, 50 years later, the visitors are still keeping tabs on him. "Too many strange things have happened."

YANKEE FIRSTS

*The New York Yankees are one of the most
recognizable teams in professional sports.
Did you know they were responsible for bringing these
innovations to America's favorite pastime?*

In 1929, the Yankees were one of two teams to
put numbers on the backs of players' uniforms.
(Cleveland was the other.) Originally the Yankee
players' numbers corresponded to their positions
in the batting order. That's why Babe Ruth was #3,
Lou Gehrig was #4, and so on.

In 1937, fan David Levy sustained a skull fracture
during a scuffle with Yankee Stadium ushers as
he tried to retrieve a ball hit into the stands. Levy
sued and won $7,500 . . . a decision that led to all
baseball clubs allowing fans to keep balls hit into
the stands.

In the 1960s, catcher and outfielder—and the first
African American Yankee player—Elston Howard
invented the "batting donut," the weighted ring
that all on-deck players now use to warm up.

Government Salaries

PRESIDENT:
$400,000

VICE PRESIDENT:
$235,100

SPEAKER OF THE HOUSE:
$223,500

CABINET MEMBER:
$221,400

SENATE AND HOUSE MAJORITY AND MINORITY LEADERS:
$193,400

SENATOR:
$174,000

REPRESENTATIVE:
$174,000

FIRST LADY:
$0

FAST-FOOD FOUNDERS
Taco Bell

NOW: Taco Bell serves more than 40 million customers each week in more than 7,500 restaurants in the US alone.

THEN: The fast-food taco was invented at a San Bernardino hamburger stand. Glen Bell Jr., owner of Bell's Hamburgers and Hot Dogs, was a fan of the efficient system at McDonald's—and an even bigger fan of Mexican food. He believed fast-food tacos could give burgers "a run for their money." But the standard soft tortilla shells took too long to prepare. So in 1951, Bell came up with a nifty idea: he created a crispy fried taco shell that could be stuffed quickly. His first customer finished a taco and came back for another . . . even though that first one had dripped sauce all over his shirt and tie.

Bell's 19-cent tacos were so popular that, by 1954, he decided to sell only Mexican food. He started restaurants Taco Tia and El Taco with partners, but finally decided to go it alone. In 1962, with $4,000, Bell opened the first Taco Bell in Downey. By the time he sold the company to PepsiCo in 1978, there were 868 Taco Bells across the country. Bell's biggest claim to fame may be that he gets credit for introducing most Americans to their first taco.

POLITICIANS SPEAK

It's true hard work
never killed anybody, but I figure
why take the chance?

—RONALD REAGAN

The One and Only Funk Brothers

What do nearly all the great Motown songs have in common? The backing band, known as the Funk Brothers. These little-known studio musicians stood behind Motown greats from 1959 until 1972, when Motown Records moved from Detroit to Los Angeles. The thirteen recognized members of the band—mostly local, and mostly African American—have received little personal acclaim for their work, but members played on every one of the more than 100 Motown singles to reach #1 on the R&B charts, including iconic songs like "My Girl," "The Tears of a Clown," and "I Heard It through the Grapevine." They were honored with a Grammy Lifetime Achievement Award in 2004.

Pop Warner

In early 1929, a factory in a seedy section of Philadelphia enlisted Joseph J. Tomlin to do something about the teen vandalism it was experiencing. Within its first month of operation, 100 of its windows had been broken by juvenile delinquents who hung out in an adjacent lot and threw rocks for fun. Other factories in Philadelphia had the same problem, so Tomlin decided to get the owners together to fund a youth football league, hoping to keep those kids occupied (as well as provide them a place to channel all that aggressive energy). It worked. By fall 1929, the four-team Junior Football Conference hit the gridiron, and by 1933 it had expanded to 16 teams. That same year, veteran college football coach Glenn "Pop" Warner moved to Philadelphia to take a job as head coach at Temple University. Tomlin met Warner and asked him to speak at a JFC training clinic. On the day of the clinic, in April 1934, a nasty storm hit Philadelphia, and out of the dozen or so coaches that Tomlin had asked to speak, only Warner showed up. He lectured the 800 young football players who attended (and answered all their questions) for two hours. At the end of the night, Tomlin—following a vote by the players— renamed the league, changing it from the Junior Football Conference to the Pop Warner Conference. By the end of the decade, more than 150 teams were competing in the Pop Warner league, and it soon spread across the country as the "Little League" of football.

Surviving Prohibition

Some of the biggest American breweries around today were also the biggest American breweries around in January 1920, when Prohibition went into effect. How did they survive until repeal in 1933, and live to brew again? Many of them made "near-beer," a drink that tasted like beer but had an alcohol content lower than 0.5 percent. They also produced a beer derivative called malt syrup—a concentrated beer flavoring intended for home baking, but which could be used to make beer at home (wink, wink). Some breweries got more creative: Coors utilized clay deposits near its Colorado headquarters to start a ceramics division. Pabst made cheese. Miller (barely) survived through real-estate sales and investments. Yuengling— today the nation's oldest active brewery—produced ice cream. And Anheuser-Busch made a wide array of grocery items, including infant formula and carbonated coffee . . . and they also manufactured police vans that Prohibition officers could use to gather up bootleggers and moonshiners.

WHY'D THEY CALL IT THAT?

Grand Teton National Park, Wyoming

The names of some National Park features are rooted less in the divine and more in comedy. Grand Tetons is French for big, um, *tetons*—the French word for "breasts." The rough, jagged mountains were named by French trappers who obviously had been without the company of women for too long.

Keep Smiling

There are few advertising images more iconic than the yellow smiley face. But who knew that something intended to simply spread a little cheer could end up generating so much controversy?

In 1963, Harvey R. Ball, a World War II veteran and graphic artist, received a commission from the State Mutual Life Assurance Company, who wanted to boost company morale. Ball's grinning brainchild: a yellow circle with black eyes and a black smile. He came up with the design in about 10 minutes and received $45 for his work of art, and the insurance company emblazoned it

on posters, buttons, and signs—the jury's out on whether employees ended up smiling more, but the image did become wildly popular.

But neither Ball nor State Mutual trademarked or copyrighted the design. When Bernard and Murray Spain, owners of two Philadelphia-area Hallmark shops, appropriated the design and added the slogan "Have a Happy Day," they were able to copyright the smiling yellow face in 1971. Not only did they make a tidy profit on the novelty items they produced with the icon, they also publicly took credit for its creation.

In 1972, meanwhile, French journalist Franklin Loufrani became the first person to register the yellow smiley face for commercial use, in the newspaper *France Soir*. He then trademarked what he named "Smiley" in more than 100 countries and started the Smiley Company, which today is one of the top 100 licensing companies in the world. The Smiley Company denies Ball's origination of the mark and maintains that the smiley face is so basic, it can't be credited to anyone in particular. Despite this supposed stance, when Walmart started using the smiley face as its corporate logo in 1996, the Smiley Company launched a lawsuit that lasted a decade and cost both companies millions. (Settlement details remain undisclosed.)

Famous Last Words

*What some well-known Americans had to say
with their final breaths.*

JOHN ADAMS, US PRESIDENT
"Thomas Jefferson survives." (He didn't know that
Jefferson had died earlier the same day.)

ETHAN ALLEN, AMERICAN REVOLUTIONARY WAR GENERAL
In response to an attending doctor who attempted to
comfort him by saying, "General, I fear the angels are
waiting for you": "Waiting are they? Waiting are they?
Well, let 'em wait."

P. T. BARNUM, ENTREPRENEUR
"How were the receipts today at Madison Square Garden?"

AMELIA EARHEART, AVIATOR
In a letter to her husband before her last flight: "Please
know that I am quite aware of the hazards. Women
must try to do things as men have tried." Final radio
communication before her disappearance: "KHAQQ
calling Itasca. We must be on you, but cannot see you. Gas
is running low."

THOMAS ALVA EDISON, INVENTOR
"It is very beautiful over there."

BENJAMIN FRANKLIN, AMERICAN STATESMAN AND INVENTOR
"A dying man can do nothing easy."

No Great Leap

It's common knowledge that when the Great Depression began with the stock market crash of October 1929, dozens of broke investors jumped to their deaths from Wall Street skyscrapers. Except . . . they didn't. On the day of the plunge, a visiting German scientist *fell* out of a 16th-floor window of the Savoy Plaza Hotel near Central Park. That news was reported along with all the bad financial news. The two events became so linked in the public consciousness that an often-seen protest sign following the Great Recession of 2007 read "Jump, you [censored]."

VOTE FOR VERMIN!

A Massachusetts man who goes by the name Vermin Supreme has run—as a Democrat, a Republican, and a Libertarian—in several state and national elections since the 1980s, most recently for president in 2020. If you think the world's weird now, imagine what it could be like if President Supreme (who always wears a boot on his head and carries a large toothbrush) ever got to deliver on these actual campaign promises:

* Give every American a free pony.

* Convert to a "pony-based economy."

* Legalize human meat.

* Make crime against the law.

* Harness zombie power using the latest in hamster-wheel technology.

* Mandatory dental hygiene.

* Travel back in time and kill Adolf Hitler.

* Give all sick people a bus ticket to Canada.

* Gradually dismantle the government.

The Measure of Success

Fannie Farmer was born in Boston in 1857. After a stroke at age 16 left her partially paralyzed, she was unable to continue her education—but she was able to cook. When she was 30, she enrolled in the Boston Cooking School, where she learned about the "domestic sciences," including cooking, home management, sanitation, and nutrition. She did so well that she was hired as a teacher, and then became the principal and an author of cookbooks. Her first—and most famous—was *The Boston Cooking-School Cook Book*, published in 1896. It contained more than 1,800 recipes, but most important, it formalized measurements, using standardized cups and spoons, whereas previous cookbooks described measurements as estimates such as "a piece of butter the size of an egg." The publishers didn't think it would do well, so they made Farmer pay for the initial run of 3,000 copies. As a result, she retained copyright, and most of the profits. Lucky for Farmer. The book drew tremendous acclaim and eventually sold millions of copies, becoming the essential reference for American home cooks. It came to be known as the Fannie Farmer cookbook (later editions were actually retitled *The Fannie Farmer Cookbook*), and has remained in print for more than 120 years.

Stripped Away

Strip malls: they're a quintessential part of the American landscape, thanks to Los Angeles. The city's famous car culture started in the 1920s, when the price of automobiles dropped enough to allow widespread ownership. People wanted to do everything in their cars, and in 1924 the first "drive-in market" opened in Glendale. These convenience stores were located at busy intersections; patrons could park in front, grab a couple things, and quickly be on their way. Those stores became the anchors of small shopping centers. There were 250 drive-in markets in Southern California by the end of the 1920s, just as supermarkets became popular . . . and started replacing drive-ins. Strip malls (or mini-malls) reemerged in 1973, again in Los Angeles, and again because of cars. Gas shortages led to hundreds of gas stations closing, and real-estate developers replaced them with a row of retail stores housing nail salons, restaurants, dry cleaners, doughnut shops, and laundromats. (Just like in the 1920s, parking was free, plentiful, and close.) The first modern strip mall was built on the corner of Osborne Street and Woodman Avenue in Panorama City; by the mid-1980s, Southern California was home to 3,000 mini-malls. (By 2010, there were more than 60,000 of them across the United States.)

STRANGE TRIP

THE DEVIL'S ROPE MUSEUM

LOCATION: McLean, Texas

DETAILS: If you've ever spent your days pondering the myriad uses and types of barbed wire (more than 2,000 kinds!), then this is the place for you. This tribute to barbed wire, which has been wrapped around ranches since 1874, is housed in an old bra factory. Inside, visitors learn that the wire was dubbed "devil's rope" because it injures so many people, livestock, and wild animals. Its other notable roles: caging prisoners, transmitting telephone signals, and planting crops—with a machine that ran along fences and dropped seeds at each barb. The museum has snagged unique samples of foreign wire crafted from camel hair and cactus stickers, as well as rare Cocklebur and Dodge Star wires, each worth hundreds of dollars . . . *per inch.*

Historical Ink

Tattoos are trendier than ever, but they're nothing new. Even these historic Americans had them.

ANDREW JACKSON (1767–1845)

Jackson's policies displaced thousands of Native Americans from their homes. Ironically, he had a tomahawk tattooed on his inner thigh.

JAMES K. POLK (1795–1849)

Tattoos of Chinese characters meaning "strength" or "peace" may be clichéd now, but the idea was very unusual when President Polk did it. He had a tattoo of a Chinese character that translates to "eager."

R. H. MACY (1822–1877)

Before he went on to found one of the nation's longest surviving department stores, Macy joined the crew of a whaling ship at age 15—which is probably when he had a red star tattooed on either his hand or forearm (accounts of its location vary). That tattoo became the inspiration for the Macy's red star logo in use today.

THOMAS EDISON (1847–1931)

The prolific inventor best known for devising the light bulb also patented an electric pen that failed as a writing instrument, but later served as the basis for Samuel

O'Reilly's invention of the electric tattoo needle. So it's fitting that Edison himself had a tattoo: five dots in a quincunx pattern (four dots forming a square, with a fifth in the center) on his forearm.

THEODORE ROOSEVELT (1858–1919)

The rugged president was a pioneer of modern masculinity, including tattoos. As a young man, he had the Roosevelt family crest inked onto his chest.

BARRY GOLDWATER (1909–98)

The US senator from Arizona and father of modern conservatism got a crescent moon and four dots tattooed on his hand. It's the symbol of the Smoki People, an Arizona group dedicated to preserving southwestern Native American history.

GEORGE P. SHULTZ (1920–2021)

Shultz had a distinguished career as Secretary of Labor and Secretary of the Treasury under President Nixon, and as Secretary of State under President Reagan. He also had a tattoo of a tiger—the mascot of his alma mater, Princeton University—on his butt.

JIM WEBB (B. 1946)

The former Secretary of the Navy and former Democrat senator from Virginia is also a decorated Vietnam veteran—and a tattoo enthusiast. Webb has three tattoos, all celebrating his Irish and Scottish ancestry.

A PERFECT SCORE

In 2011, after 29 years of coaching at Erasmus High School in Brooklyn, New York, Vic Butler retired. His win-loss record as a basketball coach wasn't particularly impressive. His greatest accomplishment: every single varsity player he coached—all 400 of them—not only graduated, but made it into some kind of secondary education. Butler's rules were strictly enforced: If a player's grades slipped, or he got into disciplinary trouble, he was suspended. If a player failed to submit college applications and financial-aid forms on time, he was suspended. His tough approach worked. "I still think about the lessons I learned from Coach almost every day," Ray Abellard told the *New York Daily News*. Abellard graduated in 1999 and now runs a basketball camp in the neighborhood. "It's nice to win," added Butler, "but the most important thing is to do well in school. I always taught the kids that basketball is just a vehicle for getting where you need to go in life."

TAKE A LEFT ON STRANGE STREET

Bored with your ho-hum street name?
Consider relocating to one of these
real American roads.

LIQUID LAUGHTER LANE (Columbia, MD)

100 YEAR PARTY COURT (Longmont, CO)

BUCKET OF BLOOD STREET (Holbrook, AZ)

ANYHOW LANE (Gansevoort, NY)

TATER PEELER ROAD (Lebanon, TN)

CHICKEN GRISTLE ROAD (Granbury, TX)

WEINER CUTOFF ROAD (Weiner, AR)

UPTHA ROAD (Casco, ME)

HAVITURE WAY (Eugene, OR)

STUBBORN GERMAN COURT (Fairbanks, AK)

THIS AIN'T IT ROAD (Dadeville, TN)

ZZYZX ROAD (Zzyzx, CA)

FARFROMPOOPEN ROAD (Constipation Ridge, AR)

POLITICIANS

SPEAK

Is the country

still here?

—CALVIN COOLIDGE, waking up from a nap

STRANGE TOWN NAMES *(Answers for page 20.)*

g – Accident, Maryland

d – Bat Cave, North Carolina

j – Boring, Oregon

a – Normal, Illinois

h – Peculiar, Missouri

b – Random Lake, Wisconsin

f – Santa Claus, Indiana

c – Dish, Texas

e – Funk, Nebraska

i – Hurt, Virginia

SHOOT ON A SHINGLE *(Answers for page 123.)*

1.	a	6.	m	11.	k
2.	e	7.	h	12.	c
3.	b	8.	n	13.	l
4.	i	9.	g	14.	f
5.	d	10.	j		

YOU HAVE DIED OF DYSENTERY *(Answers for page 216–217.)*

1. c – There are six states along the Oregon Trail: Missouri, Kansas, Nebraska, Wyoming, Idaho, and Oregon.

2. b – The first wagon train left Elm Grove, Missouri, on May 16, 1842. Approximately 1,000 pioneers made the journey. Although they were the first organized group to make it from Missouri to Oregon, they weren't the first travelers along the Oregon Trail: fur trappers had been using the trail since the early 1800s.

3. b – In 1843, residents living in the area that became Oregon decided to offer free land to anyone who would farm it. Single people could claim 320 acres; married couples, 640. Land claims remained free until 1854, when Oregon Territory officials changed the laws. New residents now had to pay for a farm, but it was still affordable: Oregon's fertile fields went for $1.25 per acre. (If you were thinking gold in California was the main reason, you weren't far off; the 1849 gold rush was the second most important force driving people west via the Oregon Trail.)

4. d – Pioneers on the trail had to pack smart and bring along only the essentials. Most travelers carried the following: flour, cornmeal, sugar, bacon, coffee, dried fruit, salt, tea, rice, baking soda, and beans. They brought a gun to stave off bandits and for hunting fresh

more answers next page ⟶

game, and they packed it all into a prairie schooner, the most modern wagon of the time. But even with all these packing tips, most travelers overloaded their wagons and thus walked all the way to Oregon.

5. d – The 2,170-mile trek took an average of four to six months to complete. Travelers needed to leave Missouri in April or May so they would be sure to avoid winter weather in Oregon's Cascade and Blue Mountains ranges.

6. b – Wagon accidents, drownings, bad weather, and many other hazards awaited travelers on the Oregon Trail, but the most disastrous was cholera. At the time, there was no cure for the disease, and cholera killed more people on the trail than anything else. Some wagon trains lost as many as two-thirds of their travelers to cholera.

7. c – Contrary to popular belief, attacks were rare on the Oregon Trail. In fact, many travelers reported friendly encounters with Native Americans—the Cheyenne and Pawnee often helped round up loose cattle or pull wagons out of ditches. Losing one's oxen, however, was a real possibility, and the pioneers circled their wagons in an effort to keep their livestock from wandering off.

8. c – Completion of the transcontinental railroad in 1869 made the Oregon Trail obsolete, as rail travel replaced wagon trains as the preferred method of transportation to the West.

9. a – Between 1841 and 1867, approximately 350,000 people made the journey from the Midwest to Oregon's Willamette Valley; it was one of the largest migrations in American history.

10. d – Congress established the Oregon National Historic Trail in 1978. Today, US Route 26 follows much of the route of the Oregon Trail.

TOO CLEVER FOR WORDS *(Answers for page 321.)*

1. Igloo: it's shaped like a hemisphere and, obviously, appears in the north.

2. Octopi: they have a lot of arms.

3. Oleo: "oleo" is margarine; you put a pat of it on a bun.

4. Bio: a "bio" tells the story of someone's life and preserves it for posterity.

5. Autos: these make traffic jams.

6. Cell: a "cell" is where a criminal goes after sentencing.

INDEX of STORIES

INDEX OF STORIES

INDEX OF STORIES

INDEX of STORIES

INDEX of STORIES

INDEX OF STORIES

Look for other titles in this successful series!

Available in printed and e-book formats.

Strange History

Mysterious artifacts, macabre legends, kooky inventions, reality-challenged rulers, boneheaded blunders.

Strange Science

Earth-shattering eurekas, outlandish inventions, silly "scientific" studies, and the stories behind the weirdos who made it all happen.

Strange Crime

Dumb crooks, celebrities gone bad, unsolved mysteries, curious capers, odd laws, and more.

Strange Hollywood

Amazing and intriguing stories about movies, music, and pop-culture phenoms, from Tinseltown and beyond.

Get Connected

Find us online to sign up for our email list, enter exciting giveaways, hear about new releases, and more!

Website: www.portablepress.com

Facebook: www.facebook.com/portablepress

Pinterest: www.pinterest.com/portablepress

Twitter: @Portablepress

Instagram: @Portablepress